Tales from the Haunted South

THE STEVEN AND JANICE BROSE LECTURES
IN THE CIVIL WAR ERA

William A. Blair, editor

The Steven and Janice Brose Lectures in the Civil War Era are published by the University of North Carolina Press in association with the George and Ann Richards Civil War Era Center at Penn State University. The series features books based on public lectures by a distinguished scholar, delivered over a three-day period each fall, as well as edited volumes developed from public symposia. These books chart new directions for research in the field and offer scholars and general readers fresh perspectives on the Civil War era.

Tales from the
Haunted
South

Dark Tourism and

Memories of Slavery from

the Civil War Era

TIYA MILES

The University of North Carolina Press *Chapel Hill*

*This book was published with the assistance of the
Fred W. Morrison Fund for Southern Studies of the University of
North Carolina Press and the George and Ann Richards
Civil War Era Center for the Brose Lecture Series.*

Designed by Alyssa D'Avanzo
Set in Utopia by codeMantra, Inc.

Manufactured in the United States of America

The paper in this book meets the guidelines for permanence and
durability of the Committee on Production Guidelines for Book
Longevity of the Council on Library Resources.

The University of North Carolina Press has been a member of the
Green Press Initiative since 2003.

Jacket illustration: "The Dark Lady," from The Clarence John Laughlin
Archive at The Historic New Orleans Collection, acc. no. 1983.47.4.957

Library of Congress Cataloging-in-Publication Data
Miles, Tiya, 1970– author.
Tales from the haunted South : dark tourism and memories of
slavery from the Civil War era / Tiya Miles.
pages cm — (The Steven and Janice Brose lectures in the Civil War era)
"This book was published with the assistance of the Fred W. Morrison
Fund for Southern Studies of the University of North Carolina Press
and the George and Ann Richards Civil War Era
Center for the Brose Lecture Series."
Includes bibliographical references and index.
ISBN 978-1-4696-2633-8 (cloth : alk. paper) —
ISBN 978-1-4696-2634-5 (ebook)
1. Ghosts—Southern States—History. 2. African Americans—
Southern States—History. 3. Slavery—Southern States—History.
4. United States—History—Civil War, 1861–1865. I. Title. II. Series:
Steven and Janice Brose lectures in the Civil War era.
BF1472.U6M546 2015
133.10975—dc23
2015017760

For Joseph, my steadfast traveling companion

Contents

Preface
The Haunting Blues, xi

Introduction
A Ghost Hunt, 1

1
Molly and Matilda
Old Savannah Specters, 21

2
Madame Lalaurie
French Quarter Fiend, 48

3
Chloe and Cleo
Louisiana Plantation Phantoms, 80

Conclusion
A Revisitation of Spirits, 115

Notes, 133

Acknowledgments, 149

Index, 151

Illustrations

Sorrel-Weed House, Savannah xiv

Savannah Halloween poster 3

Charleston ghost-tour brochure 8

Sorrel-Weed House brochure 34

Georgia State Historic Site sign,
Old Sorrel-Weed House 41

Marie Laveau's crypt, New Orleans 52

Haunted History Tour sign,
New Orleans 59

The Myrtles Plantation brochure, Louisiana 84

The Myrtles Plantation House,
St. Francisville 89

Chloe doll for sale at The Myrtles Plantation 106

Tour vehicles in the Savannah Visitor
Center parking lot 131

The Haunting Blues

I carried a secret in my bag when I arrived at the Savannah airport one February day in 2012. It was spring break at the midwestern university where I teach, and I was seeking the warmth of the southern sun. I was also seeking something else: inspiration—for a writing project that I had not dared tell my friends or colleagues about. I am a teacher and historical writer whose academic books have focused on black slavery among the Cherokees. At the time that I landed in Savannah, I was covertly attempting a novel. I wanted to tell a fictional story about a Cherokee plantation called Diamond Hill, the focus of my second work of history. Established by the Cherokee entrepreneur and political leader James Vann, Diamond Hill was (and still is) operated as a Georgia State Historic Site called the Chief Vann House. I had described in my work of history how James Vann's plantation was a cauldron of trouble for enslaved blacks, and now I wanted to capture the interior aspects of these individuals' lives and of their relationships with one another. Emotionally and ethically, I had never been satisfied with how the documented history unfolded for enslaved black women and Cherokee women on the Vann plantation, and through fiction, I seized the chance to write my own ending in which the characters could achieve a kind of poetic justice.

But this was all more easily imagined than carried out, I had discovered. The fictional genre was new and untested for me, and I was struggling with it. Where could I go to rejuvenate my thinking? The answer popped into my head one gray winter morning: the Hostess City of the South. I could go to Savannah, the most storied urban locale in Georgia, where genteel wealth and crushing slavery flourished together like poisonous, tropical vines. So I set out to soak in the atmosphere of a very old, knowing city, to visit historic homes where enslaved people had lived and labored, to project my imagination into the past and mount a full-scale rewrite of the secret novel. I arrived in Savannah with a draft of the manuscript, which hunched inside my bag as a set of loose dog-eared pages, just as the weather was changing for the worse. The day before had been dry and bright but not too hot, I learned from the sleek African American woman at the front desk of the Bohemian Hotel. But now rain was threatening behind a cool wind. Soon the rain made good on that threat, pouring, drizzling, and failing to stop for three days straight. I spent the first half of the dreary trip in my subdued, riverfront room, reading my fiction manuscript and looking out on the water that had once brought hundreds of slaves to this port.

The next day I ventured out despite the foul weather, walking the city in a lightweight jacket and wishing that I had packed a real coat. I carried a paltry travel umbrella and flapped around a color-coded map, making my way to the city's most esteemed historic homes on squares graced by monuments and moss-draped oaks. I tramped at least twenty blocks, then toured two exquisite mansions along with their restored slave quarters: the Greek Revival home of cotton merchant Andrew Low, the wealthiest businessman in Savannah in the antebellum period (whose daughter-in-law, Juliette Gordon Low, founded the Girl Scouts), and the Regency style Owens-Thomas House, now operated by the Telfair Museum of the Savannah School of Art and Design (or SCAD).

Nearly a decade before when I had begun my research on southern slavery, black history had been all but ignored at historic home and plantation sites. The people who had mattered in these tours were the slaveholding high-society families, not their chattel slaves. African American bondsmen and bondswomen had been transformed into virtual ghosts, absent and yet eerily present in historical tours as invisible laboring bodies that made their owners' fortunes shine. But there was little of this blatant erasure at the historic homes I visited on that chilly day. I was surprised by what I found in Savannah's historic district. The sites I toured had adjusted, if only slightly, to a shift in interpretive house museum culture spurred by the practice of social history— an academic approach to historical research and writing that focuses on everyday people and diverse social groups rather than on political leaders and the Euro-American male elite. This broadening of the historical canvas in the 1970s, '80s, and '90s had intersected with the rise of ethnic studies, including African American studies, a field that had produced a number of critical evaluations of the lack of portrayals of slave experience at plantation sites. In addition, house museum culture was shifting in response to a new standard articulated by the National

Park Service in the report *Imperiled Promise: The State of History in the National Park Service* (2011), which stressed, among other principles, the need for historic sites to "expand interpretive frames" and "forthrightly address conflict and controversy both in and about the past."[1]

Likely as a result of these higher expectations for broader and more realistic representation in historical accounts, the Low and Owens-Thomas tours duly noted the presence of black slaves. Nevertheless, the interpretation offered to the public was less than satisfying at the Low House, where enslaved people were referred to only briefly and by the sanitized term "servants," and where tour guides represented slaves, either optimistically or disingenuously, as adopted members of their white owners' families. (At the Low House, a black man named Tom who worked as the butler and house manager for the wealthy cotton merchant family was said to have been the dear friend of his master. Yet Low left Tom behind to manage the house in the dreaded damp heat of summer while the Low family fled to northern Georgia or England to bask in cooler climes, ensuring their safety from yellow fever.) At the second site I visited that day, the Owens-Thomas House, African American experience was more rigorously interpreted, to the extent that the faint tone of "haint blue" paint clinging to the preserved slave-quarter ceiling was described to the crowd as the color slaves preferred for warding off evil spirits.[2]

After the tours I had a late lunch in the darkened tavern of the 17Hundred90 Inn, poring over my walking-tour guidebook to historic Old Savannah.[3] I propelled myself out of the tavern and into the damp chill of the day, starting back toward the hotel by way of the narrow, eighteenth-century streets. I would have passed right by the Sorrel-Weed House. I had never heard of the place. But as I wended my way through the gray gardens of Madison Square, I saw a woman waving to me. "Would you like to take a historic tour of the Sorrel-Weed House?" she called. Her voice dipped at the end, a subtle seduction. This was the first instance during my time in Savannah that I had been actively solicited to tour a historic home. I was intrigued by the thought of it, of being beckoned into history, and I was curious about the carefree air of the solicitor. The woman could have been plucked right out of a SCAD classroom, and probably had been. With her preternaturally tinted hair and dark, sleek jeans, she looked like a stylish part-timer, a historic homes dilettante who would rush back to her art studio to set stones into jewelry as soon as

Sorrel-Weed House, Savannah, Historical American Buildings Survey, 1936.
This grand Greek Revival home, photographed in 1936, was occupied by the
Sorrel family in the antebellum era. The home is a Georgia State Historic Site
located in a National Historic Landmark district. Library of Congress,
Prints & Photographs Division, HABS GA, 26-SAV, 48—1.

the last group of tourists had departed. She reeled me in. I bought a
ticket, approaching the house that was visually imposing and somehow strange beneath its coat of peeling blood-orange paint.

Inside a long and empty hallway, I scanned my surroundings. The
Sorrel-Weed appeared at first like any other historic home open for
tours in the city, but there were subtle signs of neglect that gave it the
feel of being in mourning: a roped-off second story, a faint musty smell,
and antique furnishings with threadbare upholstery. A young man
called me into the parlor, where a pleasant older white couple sat on
a sofa waiting for the late afternoon tour to begin. They made small
talk, mentioning that they were visiting from a neighboring southern
city. We were a tiny tour group of only three. It was the slow season in
Savannah. The tourists would pour in as the weather warmed, filling
the museums of the historic district and nearby popular Tybee Beach
with color, sound, and cheer. Our animated tour guide made up for our
small number with a tongue-in-cheek enthusiasm. Dark haired and
boy-band handsome, he was quick on his feet and possessed a witty,

effortless intelligence. The gothic historical narrative that he spun for us was equal parts enthralling and outrageous.

Our tour guide told us that Francis Sorrel, a French cotton merchant, had built this house back in the 1830s. One of the richest men of his time, Sorrel had reveled in flaunting his wealth. He commissioned elaborate fireplaces and ceiling medallions, still preserved in the home, and hosted lavish parties that spilled out onto Madison Square. He owned twenty-five Haitian slaves; but he only needed five to run the household, so he gave the others four days off per week. But Sorrel had a secret. He possessed one-fourth black Haitian blood. The cotton tycoon was passing for white in Savannah high society. In order to hide his racial identity, he developed strategies to emphasize his wealth. He always arrived late to his own parties, for instance, to allow his guests time to soak in the grandeur of his home. The only sign of Sorrel's true ancestry was to be found in the private dining room. Here, where Sorrel and his white wife, Matilda, dined, Sorrel's Afro-Caribbean heritage broke out of hiding—in the pineapple plaster-ceiling motif, bright coral wall color, and curved walls where corners should have been. A superstitious man due to his Haitian roots, Francis Sorrel believed in ghosts and thought they lurked in corners. He always ate with his back to the curved walls, leaving his fragile wife to sit with her back to the remaining corners of the rectangular dining room.[4]

Our tour guide led us to the basement of the home, which he said housed the slaves' recreational room, where they enjoyed hot running water from a pipe behind the fireplace, a luxury that most Savannahians, white or black, lacked. Next to the slaves' room there was evidence that Francis may have practiced Voodoo, our guide confided. Chicken and goat bones had been discovered below the doorframe, and human remains had been found beneath the floorboards. No one really knew to whom those bones belonged. Were they the remains of Sorrel's slaves? Or could they be those of Revolutionary War soldiers killed in a battle that had taken place in the immediate vicinity of Sorrel's land?

The Sorrel home was shrouded by tragedy, our tour guide continued. Sorrel's first wife had died of yellow fever. His second wife, her sister, had committed suicide by jumping off the second-floor balcony and landing on her head in the courtyard below. Why did she jump? Because Sorrel was having an affair with Molly, a slave girl, in the slave quarters of the carriage house. One day Matilda had caught the pair in the act, and she could not live with Francis's betrayal. A week after Matilda's death,

Molly was found strangled, dangling from the ceiling rafters of the carriage house. Foul play was suspected. Did Francis kill Molly out of guilt, shame, or an attempted cover-up of the affair? Or did the other slaves murder her because of her traitorous involvement with the master? Answers to these questions have never been settled. After the deaths of both women, Francis moved next door into a tall townhouse with very few windows. He built a brick wall between his old and new properties and resided in the townhouse until his death at age seventy-seven. Sorrel lived much longer than the norm for men of his time. The belief was that he might have tried to achieve eternal life through Voodoo rituals involving human sacrifice—exchanging the life force of younger men of similar size for his own extended years. Molly and Matilda were still present on the grounds as ghosts who haunted the premises. If we wanted to see the carriage house where Molly had died and hear the supernatural story of the Sorrel-Weed House, our guide told us, we could return in the evening for the Haunted Ghost Tour.

I listened to this story while moving through the faded rooms of the residence, envisioning the vivid events as our able tour guide narrated them. Hearing an emotionally laden tale while occupying the space where the story occurred created an intense feeling of connection and horror for me. It was as though I could see right through the walls of this house of bondage. On the other side were people trapped in an intimate triangle of corruption made possible and authorized by the system of chattel slavery: Molly, a young woman of African descent who had everything stolen from her; Matilda, a privileged white mistress nevertheless subject to her husband's authority; and Francis, the French patriarch and cotton merchant of color who abused others and had perhaps himself suffered from the ignominy of his racial identity in a white supremacist social structure. The sordid tale, and the sense of intensity created by the holistic tour experience, left me feeling disturbed and uneasy. The presentation was too raw and also withholding, realistic in some aspects but inauthentic in others. I felt overwrought and at the same time deeply distrustful of the Sorrel-Weed House historic tour. I hurt for Molly. I pitied Matilda. I was enraged at Francis Sorrel. I could not let the terrible story go.

But our tour guide could. With his narrative concluded, he led us promptly to the door, thanking us with an easy smile. The older couple exited. I hung back to ask a few questions. What evidence did the site staff have that these events had actually taken place? How did they know about Molly and Matilda, about the relationships and the deaths? The tour guide told me the homeowner had found ample information in a collection of Civil War letters. I asked how I might follow up to learn more. He held out a business card (not for the historic site, but for his own rock band) and ushered me from the building.

I left with all of my plans set askew for how I would spend the remainder of my visit to Savannah. The fiction manuscript would have to be put aside to make room for the Sorrel-Weed House. I knew I would be back that night for the evening ghost tour. I did not suspect then what I know now, however: that Francis Sorrel's Savannah mansion was nothing more than a house of cards, haunted by the lingering ghosts of American slavery. Or that in the landscape of southern "dark tourism," it was not alone.

Tales from the Haunted South

A Ghost Hunt

You crave to let history haunt you as a ghost or ghosts,
with the ungraspable incorporation of a ghostly body.
—Gayatri Chakravorty Spivak, "Ghostwriting" (1995)

❧✦❧

Grasping at Ghosts: First Pursuits of the Paranormal

The Sorrel-Weed House Ghost Tour in Savannah was my initiation into the subculture-turned-megaculture of paranormal pursuits. Before stepping into that eerie home, I had steered clear of the supernatural beyond the realm of African American literature, where ghosts, indeed, abound. I hedged my bet that ghosts don't exist in the real world by avoiding them just in case they did. Somewhere along the way of my African American midwestern upbringing, I had picked up an unequivocal message: don't mess with the spirit world, and it won't mess with you. My great-grandmother Anna Christian had a cryptic saying that I now interpret as crystallizing this notion. "Never cross water," she used to command, warning her grandchildren enigmatically as she rocked, sightless, in her chair beside a window of my grandparents' house. I did not know this great-grandmother, and I can't say that I fully grasp precisely what she meant by this language. Nor, I suspect, did my mother or aunt, who shared Anna Christian's words with me years later when I was a young girl. But as I embarked on this quest, my great-grandmother's saying returned to my mind. I gathered, upon reflection, that Anna Christian meant this: there is a line between the spirit realm and our realm. It is fluid. Beware.

So I was wary when I realized that in order to pursue my burning questions about Molly, the enslaved young woman rendered ghostly at the Sorrel-Weed House, I would have to delve into the paranormal world of ghost hunting. My only sister was wary too. During the winter

1

holiday break when I was set to return to the South to visit a series of haunted sites, my sister begged me not to go. We had been raised in a small Black Baptist church on the outskirts of Cincinnati, where we had been taught to avoid the signs and symbols of spiritual danger. Although we had both attained college educations and now moved in professional circles—she in banking and I in academia—we were still superstitious about these formative teachings and warnings. My sister pleaded with me to cancel my trip as we stood in the living room of my father and stepmother's suburban house, and then, watching my face, she relented. "If you have to go," she said, "and if you see *anything*, rebuke it in the name of Jesus Christ. I'm telling you, Tiya. Rebuke it."

But my sister's attempt to keep me safe and to keep all manner of ghosts at bay was fruitless in our present moment when the cultural phenomenon of ghosts and haunting has thickened like a fog. Televised ghost stories and visits to haunted sites have grown in frequency, density, and popularity in American culture since at least the early 2000s. Now what I have come to call "ghost fancy" is a cultural tsunami fed by new, mostly digital technology; reality and dramatic TV series about ghosts and other undead creatures (vampires, zombies, demons); local paranormal hobbyist groups; books; websites; social media spaces; and a plethora of ghost tours. Travel—touristic travel in particular—emerged as a central feature of the ghost hunting experience. Professional and amateur hunters alike journeyed to novel locations across the country, such as rural farmhouses and scenic lighthouses, insane asylums and military barracks, to track down spirits of the dead. The colorful regional contexts of these sites (local history, community customs, natural beauty, and architectural landmarks) formed intriguing backdrops for paranormal investigations. In 2010 the *Huffington Post* chronicled the "Seven Best Ghost and Paranormal Shows," ranking the Travel Channel's "Ghost Adventures" as number 1.[1] Hit television series such as *Ghost Hunters* on the Syfy Channel (2002–present) and *Supernatural* on the CW Network (2005–present) featured hunky (mostly white, male, working-class) ghost busting teams taking what could be viewed as the iconic American road trip. The guys fanned out around the country in buffed black American-made vehicles (in one case vintage, in another brand new), their trunks packed with high-tech equipment and holy water. Viewers could go along for the virtual ride and, increasingly, plan their own ghost-themed trips or, for the less diehard enthusiasts, add an element of mystery to any vacation by slotting in

Savannah Halloween poster. This campy ghost-tour advertisement found online by the author in 2013 plays with the notion of spooky Savannah at Halloween.

a prepackaged ghost tour. At the turn of the twenty-first century and into the next decades, Americans became obsessed with spirits of the dead and joined that fascination with an equally intense appetite for traveling "outside their usual environment." The search for ghosts and a quest for novelty went hand in glove at a moment when tourism was steadily rising to become a multitrillion-dollar global industry.[2]

In order to find Molly, I would have to dive into that moment and immerse myself in ghost fancy. My first step was to gain a practical foundation by studying the tricks of the ghost hunting trade. I started by ordering a basic how-to guide online: *The Everything Ghost Hunting Book*. It was here that I learned the essential lingo. EVP stands for electronic voice phenomena, which are sounds emitted by spirits on a frequency beyond that of human hearing. Through the use of audio recording, particularly digital recording, voices could be captured, analyzed, and disseminated. EMF meters are devices that measure the electromagnetic frequency in an area, lighting up in response to fluctuations in the electromagnetic field. Because ghosts are made of energy and require energy to materialize on our plane of existence, these meters can spike when a spirit is near, even if that spirit's presence cannot be discerned by human senses. Infrared thermal meters read and reflect the temperature in an area, indicating the presence of cold spots that could mean a spirit has entered that spatial zone, sucking the air around it of the energy that sustains heat. And orbs are circles of light, sometimes bright white, sometimes colored, that are caught on camera. Orbs can indicate the presence of spirits invisible to the photographer or videographer in real time. A serious ghost hunter, though, must take care with the interpretation of orbs, as sometimes orbs are just flecks of dust or flashes of light. It is the orb that seems to move across a digital screen with a humanlike intentionality, or the orb that glows in radiant hues of blue or violet, that is most likely to be a spirit.

After getting the lingo (nearly) down, I turned to reading published accounts of southern ghost stories, often printed by local presses and niche presses that specialize in the paranormal. I focused on Savannah, the site of the Sorrel-Weed haunting that had propelled my research quest. I learned from *Savannah Spectres and Other Strange Tales* (a classic book in the genre published in 1984 and reprinted sixteen times since) and other books like it, such as *Savannah Hauntings* and *Georgia Ghosts* (this list could go on and on), that ghost stories of Savannah as well as other southern locales proliferate.[3] Readers pick up these published accounts at tourist stops and in local bookstores, as well as online, often as an accompaniment to their vacations down South.

A final step I took in preparation for my pursuit was talking to scholars and tourism industry first-adopters who had greater experience than I on the subject of haunted historic sites. It was fortuitous that I had been invited to offer a keynote lecture at the Southern American Studies Association conference, which met in Charleston, South Carolina, in 2013. The conference featured a threaded session on the subject of "the Spectral South," which helped to shape my early questions and, as a bonus, brought me to scenic Charleston, ranked as the number 1 tourist destination in the country at the time.[4] Before setting out, I emailed Geordie Buxton, author of the intriguing *Haunted Plantations: Ghosts of Slavery and Legends of the Cotton Kingdom*. Published in 2007, the book recounted ghost lore from plantations, brick kilns, and watery graves linked to slavery in the Charleston area.[5] I told Buxton about my interest in black ghosts at historic sites and asked to reserve a ticket for his ghost tour. He said it was the slow season, so he was on hiatus, but he offered to give me a personalized ghost tour combined with local African American history highlights. If I liked it, he asked in return that I give him a positive rating on Trip Advisor.

I met Geordie Buxton in the lobby of the historic Francis Marion Hotel on King Street. A Charlestonian from birth with dark curly hair and hazel eyes, he had the look of someone who has hiked the Appalachian Trail. His personal style gave the impression that ghost touring was an adventurous and daring activity. We left the hotel, which Buxton told me had been built with federal money intended to boost the city's fortunes after the Civil War, and headed down the narrow streets. We stopped in front of the gorgeous Aiken-Rhett House, a grand manor home built of stucco and brick with full-length, painted verandas. We didn't want to take the formal tour (I had been there during a previous research trip), so we paused outside the slave quarters, silently gazing at the peeling stucco walls. As we left the home, Buxton suggested that instead of walking the route of the ghost tour as he usually did with groups, we should take his car.

Buxton and I spent four hours touring historic Charleston on that lush January afternoon. The city pulsed with vibrant blooms and unseasonably warm sea breezes. Beautiful, aged, in-town mansions gave way to modern condominiums in a cityscape full of jarring juxtapositions. Tucked among the buildings on an undeveloped lot, the shell of a brick slave quarter stood like a ruin. Buxton told me that the intricate, sharp-tipped iron gates surrounding stately homes close to the harbor had been placed after Denmark Vesey's famous (and failed) slave rebellion of 1822. Charleston leaders had responded to the conspiracy with a ferocious backlash of punitive measures. The knife-sharp iron fence posts were meant as a warning and physical impediment to slaves who stepped out of line. If a black man or woman tried to escape the confines of the master's lot, he or she might be impaled. It was lovely but awful, that city built of ruddy bricks shaped by the hands of slaves, with its private gates pronged like spears to keep those very same slaves from escaping.

Charleston was the belle of the cultured South in the 1830s to 1850s, flush with wealth from the growth and transport of the cotton crop. "This city was a prison for the slaves," Buxton told me as he drove, "and the only British North American city to be built behind a wall." Interspersed with stories of Denmark Vesey's rebellion and minister Morris Brown's organized circle of resistant men of color, Buxton told tales of haunted plantations around the periphery of the seaport metropolis. He recounted the legend of Ibo Landing and the ghosts of slaves who rebelled on a ship, drowned in resistance, and are said to haunt the waters there. He mentioned the ghost of Drayton Hall, an iconic white-columned plantation home and historic site, which was haunted by the master's drunken son. He described the ruins of Boone Hall plantation's brick-making kiln, now half-submerged underground on the perimeter of a suburban development. A female ghost whose arms whirled in a blur of frantic motion haunted the brick kiln there. People had reported sightings of her on the roadside by the ruins, just at the falling of night. Buxton did not know who the woman was, only that she seemed tortured, caught in an endless loop of senseless labor. He speculated that she was the spirit of one of the hundreds of slaves forced to fire the bricks that had built historic Charleston.

As we navigated the city in his vintage white Saab, Buxton told me he runs three tours in Walks in History, the company that he co-owns with his brother and a third business partner. Walks in History offers a haunted tour, a pirate tour, and a Civil War history tour. Ghosts, he said, do the best by far. He was making a comfortable living giving tours and writing about local lore, even enough to get him through the slow late fall and winter season. His book *Haunted Plantations* had dramatically increased traffic on his tours. He expected that he could self-publish the new book he was writing, *Supernatural Charleston*, and earn even more to supplement his annual income. Other than the ghost tourists, most of his clients were "white middle-aged men from Ohio who just want to hear about the Civil War." Buxton lamented that he couldn't fit in more African American history, but he said the sites he was showing me in this tailor-made tour couldn't compete with tourists' desire for ghosts and Civil War canons.

When prompted, Buxton had plenty to say about his own views of ghosts in Charleston, which he described as "a beautiful place with a dark past." He said he believes in an energy related to ghosts that can affect people and that he's experienced "strange things." The haunted slave kitchen, a room in a house that his friend owns and rents out in the city, was an example. Everyone who has rented this particular room in his friend's apartment has had odd misfortunes, Buxton said. The latest renter had been sick for four days for inexplicable reasons. The energy of ghosts is active, Buxton believes, and not always or necessarily malevolent, but this reality is different from the stories that we, the living, tell about them. I asked Buxton why he writes ghost stories and why he thinks his ghost tours are popular. "We no longer allow violent treatment of oppressed people. We're PC and accepting," he told me. "So the violent desires get shifted into ghost stories." Buxton's notion that ghost stories function as projections of contemporary feelings about historical relationships resonated with my own thinking. Tales about ghosts seem to allow us to entertain the historically grounded social issues that nettle us, like race relations and slavery. But this engagement occurs at a safe distance created by the nature of a particular narrative form, that is, the ghost story, that carries with it a sense of the fantastical and the knowledge that what is said can be taken as fancy rather than fact.

I asked Buxton how their company's ghost tour had begun and whether it had changed over time. He told me the following story about a business partner (we'll call him Dean) who used to work in a cemetery. Dean was a "dark guy" with a "Goth personality" who used to dig graves and dress the dead in preparation for funerals. He relished the work and moved quickly into a supervisory position. Around 1995 or 1996, Dean was charged with training a few black men, new lower-wage hires, on how to dig the graves. But these men refused to remain in the cemetery when Dean left them to their tasks. The reason the men gave for their behavior was the need to avoid "haints." Dean didn't know what the men meant until they explained that a haint was a ghost in lowcountry Gullah and Geechee parlance, and the color "haint blue" was used to ward them off. Dean was also leading history tours at the time, and he threw in the bit about haints for the tourists. He noticed that the topic piqued his guests' interest, so he started integrating local ghost stories into his script. Dean soon had the brainchild that their company should create a tour devoted solely to ghosts, so they started one in 2003, making them the first company in Charleston to offer a ghost tour. The theme took off. Now there are multiple ghost tours running in the city, and everyone loves to end a tour "with a bang, with a ghost story," Buxton said. "It wakes people up after they've fallen asleep from the history part of the tour." Buxton confided that although ghost-tour enthusiasm had died down a bit over the last few years, it had picked right up again with the publication of his book *Haunted Plantations*.

Geordie Buxton was serious about his work. He believed in the paranormal, or mystical happenings beyond our full comprehension. He

Charleston ghost-tour brochure. This graphic ghost-tour brochure was collected among many others by the author during a trip to Charleston in 2013.

wanted to share the secret side of his city with me and with others who took his tours. He joked about "those tour guides from Baltimore who come down here and take a class" and was proud of being the real deal, an authentic, down-to-earth Charlestonian. And he was also part of a commercial industry that seemed to be piggybacking on black culture through the vehicle of the ghost tour. Even as I recognized Buxton's earnest approach to his work, I had nagging reservations about the enterprise. I wondered where those African American cemetery workers were now. Did they even know their haint blue stories had spurred a cottage tourist industry?

A few months after that trip to Charleston, I took my questions to Gettysburg, Pennsylvania, where historian Jill Titus was growing concerned about local ghost tourism. Dark-haired and laser smart with an unassuming, kind demeanor, Jill Titus was a professor at Gettysburg College who observed that ghost tours were proliferating in the historic Civil War town where she taught. Paranormal pursuits had become so pervasive in storied Gettysburg, where Abraham Lincoln drafted the Gettysburg Address and thousands of young Union and Confederate soldiers lost their lives, that Titus received an email notice announcing a new class on techniques for interacting with paranormal groups. The course was geared toward tour guides in the town, who, it was expected, would be encountering increasing numbers of ghost hunters hoping to glimpse the spirits of fallen soldiers or heroic civilians. In addition to this special training opportunity for traditional history tour guides, companies had begun to offer evening tours focused solely on paranormal Gettysburg.

Jill Titus wanted to know why visitors to nationally significant historic sites are drawn to paranormal programs and what ghost tours provide that public historians and guides at traditional historic sites do not. So she organized an expert panel on ghost tourism for the benchmark National Park Service (NPS) conference "The Future of Civil War History," held in the 150th anniversary year of the battle of Gettysburg on a chilly weekend in the early spring of 2013. The large meeting hall on the charming Gettysburg College campus was packed for the Friday evening ghost-tour panel. I was among the audience of NPS and academic historians, tour guides, teachers, and Civil War history buffs. The ghost-tour panel featured scholars in the fields of history, geography, tourism studies, and performance studies. One of the panelists, performance artist Robert Thompson, had worked as a ghost-tour guide. Another, geographer Glenn Gentry, had studied ghost-themed walking tours in Savannah. Richard Sharpley, who had flown in from England, was one of the leading thinkers in the scholarly field of dark tourism. And historian David Glassberg specialized in American historical consciousness and memory. Jill Titus would moderate and set the tone by offering her sharp analysis that ghost tours focus on escapism and voyeurism, thereby masking the state-sponsored violence of war.

In his opening remarks for the panel, Richard Sharpley gave the audience defining concepts for understanding the phenomenon of dark tourism, of which ghost tourism is a part. He explained that at the most basic level, dark tourism—the exploration of death, disaster, and suffering through travel—provides people with "a way to mediate between death and modern life." He indicated that the term "dark tourism" has been in use for twelve years and that the first seven years of research on the phenomenon had focused on categorizing different experiences along a continuum. Ghost tours, he said, were the "lighter side of death . . . a playful, frivolous end of the dark tourism spectrum." Robert Thompson agreed with Sharpley that ghost tours are "frivolous," "fun," and "silly." He added, "The metanarrative that informs the whole ghost-tour experience is that it's a game, fun, playing with the idea of truth." In addition to a good time, ghost tours offered their audiences "authenticity," Thompson pointed out. "You know you're getting a secret, off-the-map, off-the-grid, unauthorized experience." But beneath the frivolity and authenticity, he added, ghost tours were moneymaking ventures, "a purely capitalistic enterprise." Drawing from his experience of working as a ghost-tour guide, Thompson explained that ghost tours "bring more business in, increase energy, and increase people's desire to stay overnight."

Geographer Glenn Gentry had taken every ghost tour in Savannah and interviewed several tour guides in the early 2000s while researching his master's thesis, which he later published in academic journals. Gentry attributed the rise of ghost tourism in Savannah to the publication of the book *Midnight in the Garden of Good and Evil*, which endowed the small city with an atmosphere of mystery.[6] The wild success of *Midnight* inspired book-based tours of Savannah that were soon surpassed by ghost tours. In Gentry's research, which focused on the tourist experience, he found that people signed up for ghost tours for a range of reasons. Some were seeking novelty and wanted to learn history from a different angle. Some desired community and confirmation of supernatural experience. Others wanted to suspend rational belief and imagine other realms of possibility. Ghost tours, he said, "allow access to dissonant knowledge, dirty laundry, back stage." A ghost tour gave the tourist the opportunity to take control of his or her experience, Gentry explained, to interact with the tour guide in a dynamic way. Tourists could influence the trajectory of a tour, share their own stories of hauntings, and even find those stories incorporated into their tour guide's future narrative scripts. Gentry commented that during the yearlong period of his research, "it was only on ghost tours that [he] heard about black slaves and the use of carriage houses as slave quarters." He insisted that not all ghost tourism is about making money, that some Savannah tour guides valued the experience of introducing guests to the city. "Don't force ghosts into historic places," Gentry concluded poetically, "but if they whisper, let them come. . . . We should take ghost tourism seriously because others do."

David Glassberg, the only historian on the Gettysburg conference panel besides moderator Jill Titus, raised the most critical and, to my mind, satisfying questions about the ghost-tour phenomenon. He theorized that the contemporary culture of mobility of Americans means we are not attached to places enough to experience hauntings where we live. But while on vacation, Americans can visit old places and be in the midst of ghosts that stand in for our own ancestors. This experience of being connected to place through notions of ghosts while on vacation is a simplified and depoliticized version of the identification with place that used to occur when folks stayed closer to home, Glassberg explained. But adopted ancestors from distant locales, he argued, "are without politics and make no claims on the present." Glassberg wondered aloud if the NPS adoption of a social history approach that "takes the higher ground" and offers "more sophisticated histories" at sites like Gettysburg was turning some people off, such that ghost tours were popping up on the fringes of the battlefield. Finally, he asked with reserved provocation, "What are the boundaries of what is acceptable? Can we imagine a ghost tour of the Twin Towers? Or of a Native American massacre site?"[7]

David Glassberg's comments articulated concerns that I had been feeling as I listened to the panelists. It did seem that certain experiences and events of the past were off-limits, at least for now, to the "frivolous" enterprise of the ghost tour. These off-limits events were deemed too sensitive and important to narrativize in the playful jest of the ghost-tour frame. As Glassberg implied in his question about the Twin Towers, there is no ghost tour at the site of the September 11 attacks because the nature of such a tour would dishonor the lives that were lost there. However, as my tour of the Sorrel-Weed House in Savannah and plantation sites in Charleston had suggested to me, African American lives, and black slavery in particular, seemed to be fair game for the dark-tourism industry, so much so that deceased black slaves are main characters of the southern ghost tour.

After listening to the Gettysburg ghost-tour panel, I seized the chance to talk with geographer Glenn Gentry, who had studied Savannah ghost tourism in depth. I hoped to ask him about the Sorrel-Weed House and the story of Molly, the black slave ghost there. He was game for my questions and disclosed that when he did his research back in 2003, the Sorrel-Weed House had not been open for tours. He said he could have picked it out from my verbal description, though, because, "it was one of those houses that was always in poor shape despite the renovations." Next I asked him, "Why ghosts? What makes ghost tours so alluring to people?"

"They want to get behind the history," he answered, to experience the past "up close and personally."

But were ghost tourists actually getting behind the history, especially with regard to African American history? Was it a good thing for our public understanding of what happened in the past, or for our development of historical empathy, or for the character of our contemporary social relations that the ghost tour has resuscitated the slave? I was not so sure. But as someone who had been taken enough by the story of a slave girl ghost to come this far, I owed it to my own sense of integrity, as well as to experienced colleagues like Glenn Gentry and earnest tour guides like Geordie Buxton, to keep an open mind.

Ghosts of the Past: Theories on Why History Is Haunting

So what, exactly, are ghosts, and why do we court them? The need to establish this basic foundation led me into a study of the figure of the ghost and the role of haunting in American history and culture. Cultural studies scholars Maria del Pilar Blanco and Esther Peeren, coeditors of the absorbing work *Popular Ghosts: The Haunted Spaces of Everyday Culture*, provide a succinct definition of the ghostly. Ghosts, they explain, are the returned spirits of those who have died, manifested in recognizable form, such as shape, shadow, sound, or movement, to the living.[8] People who believe in ghosts (as well as a fair number of people who *say* they do not) hold a common understanding of the ghost as being a stuck, lost, and even tortured soul who returns to the material realm due to unresolved, often traumatic experiences. Ghosts emerge from the past to occupy the present in a mystical, looping cycle of appearance and disappearance. It is this quality of pseudo–time travel that led the French philosopher Jacques Derrida to identify temporal disturbance—the disruption and repetition of moments in time—as a primary characteristic of hauntings. Borrowing from the Shakespeare play in which Hamlet, Prince of Denmark, proclaims to the ghost of his father that "the time is out of joint," Derrida defines ghostly appearances as "spectral moments" that bend the segmented and chronological structure of the Western idea of time.[9] Transgressing temporal laws, ghosts emerge from the past to puncture the placidity of our present and to signal that "something is missing."[10] These unquiet souls of the dead are historical entities, fragments of the remembered past spirited into our present time in order to disrupt the Now.

It would seem, then, that ghostly visitors from the past fascinate us in large part because we mortal human beings are historically minded, historically grounded, and historically driven. We are drawn to discover what took place before our own appearance in the great worldwide drama of life and to speculate about what transpires once a life has been physically extinguished. Knowledge of history—often personal and family history—is so compelling to most living people that it is an essential aspect of identity formation and meaning-making. Historians Roy Rosenzweig and David Thelen found in a national survey of Americans that respondents "took the past personally" and experienced the past as "pervasive, a natural part of everyday life, central to any effort to live in the present." Survey respondents actively searched for patterns in the past to help shape their lives in the present.[11] Most of the people involved in the study—women and men from various regions, racial groups, and age groups—were employing the past as a resource, as a combined archive and tool kit for indexing and building their own lives. The Rosenzweig and Thelen study showed that history—events that took place before our time—shapes our individual identities as persons *in* time, as well as our collective identities as members of cultural communities and citizens of nations. Indeed, knowledge of the past gives us the collective ability to put our present into context, to imagine and plan for our future, and to make sense of our lives. Carl Becker, a historian who thought deeply about the psychological role of historical knowledge, wrote in 1932, "Without historical knowledge, this memory of things said and done, [a person's] today would be aimless and his to-morrow without significance."[12] What is more, knowledge of history magnifies the span of our human experience, multiplying the timeline of our individual lives by connecting that timeline to the lives of those who have gone before us. As slavery reparations advocate Randall Robinson has put it in a discussion of the importance of learning African history: history-making and other memory traditions are "essential to the health of any people's spirit. They are givers of collective self-worth, cheaters of mortality, binding frail, short lives in a people's epic cumulative achievement."[13] Philosopher K. Anthony Appiah expressed a similar sentiment in his analysis of the desire for individuals to craft "life-scripts," stories that unify the elements of a person's life and connect those elements to larger group narratives. "To fit into a collective history," he wrote, can satisfy "the desire for glory as one of the dominating impulses of human beings."[14]

And so we interpret our lives through the lens of the past, sometimes for better, sometimes for worse. But in this epic quest for history we encounter a fundamental challenge: the past exists on another plane of time, far away from us. We cannot fully access the past because it is no longer present. It is distant, shrouded, mysterious. To visit the past we require a sort of mental time machine, such as the feeling of transcendence that can be invoked by standing at an atmospheric historic site, viewing rare objects in a museum, reading a gripping historical study, or perhaps encountering a ghost. And of all the possible means of transport into the past, a ghostly encounter is arguably the most immediate, the most personal, and for some people, the most "real." According to Pew Research Center surveys, 18 percent of Americans claim they have seen or been near a ghost and 29 percent say they have "felt in touch with someone who has died." Citing Gallup polling, sociologist Claude Fischer notes that "over one-third [of Americans] say that they believe in the spirits of the dead coming back; about that many also say they believe in haunted houses."[15] This sense that spirits from beyond the grave can linger and return is a recurring element in American experience—indeed, in human experience. As novelist Edith Wharton wrote in the early 1900s, "Deep within us the ghost instinct lurks."[16] Sociologist Avery Gordon staked a claim for the import of haunting in her classic book *Ghostly Matters: Haunting and the Sociological Imagination*, writing, "Haunting is a constituent element of modern social life. It is neither pre-modern superstition nor individual psychosis; it is a generalizable social phenomenon of great import."[17] Strong belief in the existence of ghosts persists in American culture, and that belief does historical work.

Ghosts and the means by which we hold them in mind, ghost stories, make for a special mode of connection to the past. Since ghosts are essentially about the past—that is, historical—the modern ghost story can be understood as a popular form of historical narrative. The stories that we tell about ghosts are a method of history-making, then, a cultural process by which we create, use, and understand history. Through ghost stories we preserve important personal and collective knowledge about what took place in the past, and particularly about events in the past that we have excluded from active, embraced memory.

Although ghost stories are culturally important and revealing, they are marginal in comparison with formal types of historical narration (such as academic histories or museum exhibition catalogs). The fantastical, paranormal content of ghost stories makes them suspect in a field that values documented argumentative and interpretive claims. From their position on the margins of accepted historical narrative, ghost stories can convey fringe knowledge that is otherwise suppressed, avoided, or euphemized in public life. As literature scholar Judith Richardson has explained in her book about Hudson Valley hauntings, "Ghosts, those apparently insubstantial emanations from the past, are produced by the cultural and social life of the communities in which they appear. Ghosts operate as a particular, and peculiar, kind of social memory, an alternate form of history-making in which things usually forgotten, discarded, or repressed become foregrounded."[18] Ghost stories make it a point to render what is taboo, frightening, and alien to mainstream society. This means that the ghost story is not only a form of historical narrative; it is potentially a form of radical historical narrative that can dredge up unsettling social memories for reexamination.

In crafting and hearing stories of haunting, we conjure up and simultaneously contain the collective memories that threaten us. Ghost stories index disturbing historical happenings that have often been excluded from conscious social memory, but they also limit the full recognition of those very happenings. Because modern culture dismisses the possibility of ghosts (even while many people hold personal faith in the reality of haunting), ghost stories are taken lightly, in jest, and are viewed as primitive or playful. Revelations of historical import embedded in ghost stories are therefore dismissed as unreal. Ghost stories as a form of historical narrative therefore do double work: they call to mind disturbing historical knowledge that we feel compelled to face, but they also contain the threat of that knowledge by marking it as unbelievable. This process of pushing back and calling forth a memory might be described as "unsuccessful repression" in psychoanalytic literary and cultural studies. Literature scholar Renee Bergland explains the understanding of haunting as repression in this way: "The entire dynamic of

ghosts and hauntings, as we understand it today, is a dynamic of unsuccessful repression. Ghosts are the things that we try to bury, but that
refuse to stay buried. They are our fears and our horrors, disembodied,
but made inescapable by their very bodilessness."[19] Just as hauntings
are about the return of the past, or time "out of joint," ghost stories are
a controlled cultural medium for recognizing *trouble* in that past, for
acknowledging the complexities and injustices of history that haunt the
periphery of public life and leave a lingering imprint on social relations.

Ghosts are our guides to the troubled past, our metaphysical historical messengers, whose stories compel us to remember whether or not
we want to. These messengers come to us bearing bad news. The past,
they tell us, is a place rife with wrongs, with traumas that must be seen
in order to be expelled and injustices that must be exposed in order to
be redressed. As Avery Gordon has put it, "Ghosts are characteristically
attached to the events, things, and places that produced them in the
first place; by nature they are haunting reminders of lingering trouble."
Ghosts are our indication of historical discord and our notification,
Gordon writes, of "something-to-be-done."[20]

Ghosts loosed from a troubled, and indeed, troubling, past besiege
the American landscape. Many of us sense that we live in a haunted
country, a land of injured spirits. This is a metaphorical truth that
creeps to the surface again and again in our national literature and popular culture. As much as we long to idealize this nation as the birthplace
of freedom (and it was, on paper and for a privileged few), we are also
a country founded on the practice of indigenous erasure, illegal land
seizure, and racial slavery. This is something that Americans know and
yet struggle not to recognize. We are plagued by the memory of those
wronged on this land. Our understanding of this metaphorical reality
of haunting seeps from beneath our floodwalls of denial and shows in
our persistent stories about ghosts of the oppressed. The long tradition
in American literature and lore featuring American Indian ghosts is a
prime example. In order for American settlers to claim an authentic,
indigenous identity in a new land, Native Americans had to be symbolically killed and buried, only to return as ineffectual ghosts or to
be replaced by whites "playing Indian."[21] As Native American studies
scholars Colleen Boyd and Coll Thrush point out, the haunted Indian
burial ground is an all too familiar trope in American films and stories.[22]
The Indian cemetery stands in for a past native presence, signaling the
demise of the actual Indian, naturalizing native people as features of

an American landscape, and containing negative emotion for those who now occupy the land. The enslaved African American ghost is the Indian ghost's double. While the red ghost keeps alive the memory of Indian removal in U.S. history, representing white "terror and lament," the black ghost marks the demonic spirit of possession through which Americans transformed people into things.[23] These twin crimes against humanity—removal and slavery—form the underpinning of America's existence, which is why Renee Bergland calls "ghosts of slaves and ghosts of Native Americans" the "specters" that haunt "the American imagined national communit[y]."[24]

As our cultural practices shift, so do our haunting stories. While tales by Washington Irving and Edgar Allan Poe are still retold, ghost lore has rapidly moved into myriad cultural forms. Stories of spirits proliferate on television and the Internet and punctuate the growing branch of global leisure travel, termed dark tourism, that packages themes of death and atrocity at museums and historic sites. To quote the editors of *Popular Ghosts*, Blanco and Peeren, again: "we appear to live in an era that has reintroduced the vocabulary of ghosts and haunting into everyday life."[25] Ghost stories are omnipresent in the public domain, attached to historic sites and old, evocative places. In the U.S. South this surge in haunting tales has taken on a particular cast and often features spirits who are said to have been slaves.

If Molly of the Sorrel-Weed House is any indication, it seems that the ghosts of American slavery have yet to be exorcised 150 years after the Civil War. The presence of these spectral slaves reflects the tension endemic to the ghost story form. Historic sites that feature stories of black ghosts in bondage seek to engage and yet also avoid the troubling memory of slavery. Why? Because slavery and the racial ideology that justified the practice are cultural wounds that have never healed. Ghost stories of the enslaved dead bring those wounds to the surface of awareness, allowing tourists of the former slaveholding South to stare and pick at them. But seeing these wounds, acknowledging that they still fester, is uncomfortable in a would-be postracial society. Recognition must therefore be a *misrecognition* that diminishes the harsh realities of America's peculiar institution. Tourists and tour guides cannot deny that slavery happened, especially in the plantation-filled southern states. It is slavery, in fact—the sense of a dusty black essence in tandem with the charm of aristocratic planter life—that gives the region its special character in popular imagination. Without slavery there is no South, as a region or an idea. But if vacationing tourists must somehow confront the ugliness of slavery that repels as well as attracts their notice, they would probably rather do so from a safe emotional distance. The ghost tour, which showcases violent themes with a playful fright and wink, is therefore proving to be a popular conveyance of antebellum southern history. Tourism in the South today often relies on the appeal of the ghost story to interpret historical events, but does it evade the social criticism implicit in the presence of the oppressed slave ghost?

Ghost Writing: An Overview of Chapters and Sources

It was a lucky thing in 2013 that I received an invitation from historian Bill Blair to give the 2015 Brose Lectures at Penn State University's George and Ann Richards Civil War Center. His email presented me with the opportunity I needed to rationalize my pursuit of what was a wholly unexpected and, initially, less than reasoned quest. I now had license to pursue my obsessive search for Molly as well as my growing fascination with ghost fancy. And as a bonus, I could call it all "work": the stimulating conferences I was attending, the spooky pulp fiction I was reading, the reality TV I was watching, and the southern trips I was taking during winter breaks, spring breaks, and summer vacations. I could become an untrained, rather timid, and slightly cerebral ghost hunter, despite my religious baggage and skeptical orientation. My objective seemed straightforward at the time: to explore the cultural meanings of an American South still haunted by its history of slavery in the long aftermath of the Civil War.

This book recounts my journey to haunted sites and reports my investigation of ghost tours, ghost stories, and historical events attached to haunted places in the South. It also touches on the theme of haunting in African American cultural expression, which offers a potent counter-perspective to mainstream slave ghost tales. While I describe several sites and stories in the book, I focus on three key narratives that share a set of characteristics: the Sorrel-Weed House haunting in Savannah, the Madame Lalaurie House haunting in New Orleans, and The Myrtles Plantation haunting in St. Francisville, Louisiana. Each of these stories of slavery and haunting is linked to historic sites that are also public attractions; each story has been incorporated into the ghost-tour industry; each derives from events—real or imagined—in the antebellum period; and each has been widely popularized in contemporary cultural production, through books, oral histories, digital media, television, and legend.

This book is organized into three chapters preceded by a preface and an introduction and followed by a conclusion. Chapter 1 retraces my visits to Savannah in a discovery of how the city became so haunted and of how Molly became the Sorrel-Weed House star ghost. Chapter 2 recounts my travels to New Orleans for a series of ghost and cemetery tours and a visit to the home of the reportedly ghastly and also ghostly Madame Delphine Lalaurie. Chapter 3 explores haunted plantations in the River Road historic area of Louisiana and winds back to settle in at The Myrtles Plantation, where the specter of Chloe holds sway. The conclusion puts the aims of dark tourism in conversation with African American views of haunting found in Works Progress Administration (WPA) slave narratives from Georgia, an informal black focus group in New Orleans, and a black-owned tour company in Savannah.

Primary sources for this project include family papers and census records of southern slaveholding families whose homes are said to be haunted, WPA and full-length slave narratives, memoirs of haunted places, tourist guidebooks, and site souvenirs. Secondary sources draw from the fields of African American history, southern women's history, American studies, and tourism studies. Much of the reported material gathered in the work derives from my own observations collected on ghost tours in Georgia, Louisiana, and South Carolina over two years.[26] In penning this book, I am reaching toward an approach that I will call ghost writing, and I mean this in two senses.[27] First, I am telling, or attempting to tell, the story of phantomlike figures who cannot speak for themselves—the enslaved, the deceased, and even the imaginary. I have had to become something like a ghostwriter for them, a ventriloquist of their stories. My words and thoughts stand in for theirs, but only as projections, as approximations of what they might have felt or said. Second, since embarking on this project, I found that reality was constantly shifting under my feet. What seemed authentic was artificial. What seemed destructive was also productive. What I at first thought I knew, I did not really know at all. I found that in order to recount my journey in a manner that was faithful to my own uncertainty, I would need the ability to ghostwrite: to write, rewrite, and unwrite the stories of slave ghosts and my own interpretations of them, to circle back to places I had been to before, to leave traces along the way of ambivalence and contradiction, to let "the primeval shadows" haunt the page.[28]

In the story of my journey that follows, I explore how slave ghost tales function in southern tourism and why portrayals of enslaved black specters have been on the rise. I consider what these phantoms signal about memories of slavery in contemporary American culture and what the evocation of ghostly memory might tell us about the realities of historical slavery and gender relations. And I hope to channel the collective experience of those ancestor-spirits who lived through enslavement, both to defend their worthy honor and to salvage our own.

1

Molly and Matilda

Old Savannah Specters

How do we reckon with what modern history has rendered ghostly?
—Avery Gordon, *Ghostly Matters* (1997)

❧

Missing without a Trace: The Search for Molly

I don't believe in ghosts—not really, not rationally. But this did not stop me, on a damp winter night in 2012, from going in search of one. I had spent the afternoon alongside sundry strangers viewing historic homes on Savannah's graceful squares—grand abodes for cotton barons built in the Federal, Georgian, and Greek Revival styles back when Savannah had flourished from wealth begotten by slave labor. The homes were pristine inside and out—buffed and smooth, ringed by gardens, and stocked with fine antiques. But one structure, despite its imposing facade and impressive historic marker, had appeared to be in serious decline. The burnt-orange paint on the home's exterior peeled in ragged patches. The veranda facing the western side street lay littered with the detritus of a home renovation gone awry—forgotten raw plank boards, half-sealed paint cans, and an old radiator pushed haphazardly against the exterior wall. The foliage around the perimeter straggled about, overreaching the property line. It was here, in this faded structure known as the Sorrel-Weed House, where I had heard the story that compelled my return. It was the story of Molly, an abused black slave who was said to haunt this house of old deep in the heart of a modern city.

I returned to the historic district late that night and stood sequestered in the stucco-walled courtyard between the Sorrel-Weed main house and carriage house. All was quiet. The soles of my shoes pressed

21

into slave-made Savannah "brown bricks." I could not see out into the darkened city streets beyond. It was as though I had been transported into the temporal moment of the antebellum mansion whose 15,000 square feet of elegant bulk loomed over me. The corner estate cut so far into its block on Madison Square that it made the adjacent Victorian townhomes seem to yield, leaning ever eastward into the evening skyline.

My tour guide, a young white man, commented on how odd it was that I was the only customer that night. With his rumpled hair, loose blue jeans, and unkempt belt strap dangling from the waist, he brought to mind the character Shaggy from the children's mystery cartoon *Scooby Doo*. Nevertheless, I handed over my prepurchased ticket and followed him up to the second story of the carriage house formerly used as slave quarters. The faint glow of street lamps barely penetrated the chamber at the top of the stairs. The guide left the lights off and launched into the tale of the house. He recounted the saga of the Caribbean-born patriarch, Francis Sorrel, and his "affair" with his black Haitian "servant girl" Molly; of his wife Matilda's discovery of the affair and resulting suicide; of Molly's murder in the carriage house, likely at the hands of her master; and of the ghosts of Molly and Matilda that lingered on the grounds.

The guide followed his narration of sexual impropriety, slavery, suicide, and murder with a DVD clip from the Syfy Channel's popular reality show series *Ghost Hunters*. The clip featured the ghost hunting team of The Atlantic Paranormal Society, or TAPS, investigating the Sorrel-Weed carriage house. Using high-tech electronic equipment, the TAPS team had captured on tape the heavily accented ghostly scream of a woman being attacked. The TAPS investigators reported on the show that no other woman—no living woman—had been present at the time when the spectral voice was captured. The show featured footage of investigators interviewing individuals with firsthand knowledge of the home in order to pinpoint the source of the voice. A carpenter who had stayed in the carriage house while working on renovations said he had heard a female voice calling his name at night and expressed disgust upon hearing the woman caught on audiotape, whom he presumed to be "the slave girl that was raped up in the carriage house." The owner of the home said the tape supported "historical facts" that he was aware of regarding Francis Sorrel's "affair" with his "servant-slave" and that the sound on tape was "most probably" that slave woman "being beat." The Sorrel ghost story was becoming more gruesome in this mass-culture medium, with the tour guide's euphemistic description of an "affair" morphing into violent rape in the televised version of events.[1]

The guide stopped the DVD and announced that it was time for us to enter Molly's bedroom, the place where the "affair" had occurred and where she had been murdered. Objects were known to move in that room without human intervention, he told me. Furniture was sometimes mysteriously rearranged. My guide confided that he himself had felt the presence of Molly's spirit in the upper rooms of the slave quarters. I stood outside Molly's door, glimpsing the masked white walls, thick wood beams, and empty space pregnant with connotation. I did not cross over the threshold. The guide stood behind my back, urging me to enter. When I continued to hesitate, he told me psychics who had taken his tour had seen the figure of a black woman smiling in the shadows. The ghost of Molly, his words implied, approved of this tour, so why was I resisting? But when I still refused to enter the room out of what I felt was respect for Molly, my tour guide changed course, leading me outside.

As we reached the bottom of the carriage house steps, he said he had a treat for me. He would take me into the root cellar below the carriage house, a space that was never included on tours and had not been altered in the renovation of the building. A shot of anxiety ran down my spine, the anxiety that women walking alone on the streets at night know only too well. In the *Ghost Hunters* clip, the owner of the Sorrel-Weed House had said he found precious objects related to the home's history in that cellar. What might I find there, if I dared to look? Should I go down below with this man when only a taxi driver knew my whereabouts? My desire to know more about Molly and her life in this place warred with my sense of personal safety. The door to the cellar dug into the ground, yielding only to darkness beyond it. I did not have the courage to enter. I was a free person, and so I said no. The guide shook his head as though he could not fathom what manner of ghost tourist I was, passing up the chance to stand in Molly's room and experience the dank root cellar. Exasperated, the tour guide led me, then, into the bowels of the big house.

By the time I encountered the mansion's basement, I was on edge. The surroundings did nothing to soothe me. The basement was like an eerie stage, with black cloths suspended from ceilings, separating main rooms from anterior compartments hidden from the eye. A mounted television monitor revealed, via video feeds and blinking lights, various shadowy corners of the space. The guide asked if I had brought along my recorder

Molly and Matilda   23

to capture EVPs. At the time, I didn't yet know what an EVP was. I stood in the center of the largest room of the basement, clutching my bag to my chest. His long sigh told me that I was a disappointment. He soon gave up, led me into the main floor of the house, flipped on the lights, and allowed me the freedom to walk about as I wished. My recalcitrance had gotten the best of both of us, unexpectedly yielding a nearly unfettered private tour. I asked if I could step onto the veranda that I had seen from the street. He said it was off-limits to the public, but he indulged me anyway. I ducked outside through an oversized window in Francis Sorrel's library, since there was no door leading directly out to the porch. The guide did not follow, granting me precious solitude that made me rethink my view of him. It was there, tucked into the hip of the house, beneath the side eaves and protective overgrowth of shrubbery, that I could finally breathe that night, releasing suppressed anxiety, taking in the solemn feel of the old house and its history. I breathed in the thought of Molly, a slave girl, saddened by the travesty of her lived experience and angered by the fate of her afterlife. It seemed that she might be trapped on these grounds forever, always a slave in someone's service.

I cannot tell you that I felt Molly's presence in the stillness of that night, but I can tell you that I felt a kind of call. I felt a call to search for evidence of Molly's life in the archival rubble of urban slavery, to tell her story and redeem her spirit from the commercialized spectacle of bondage that I had witnessed. I pledged in the dark to restore her memory and her dignity, if I possibly could. But Molly would prove to be elusive, illusory, a phantom in the historical record as well as in the mansion. After that first trip to Savannah in 2012, I began my search for her with a survey of historical documents, fully expecting that the papers and records of nineteenth-century Savannah would allow me to re-create the contours of Molly's life. Because Molly was owned as an object, a person who had lived as the possession of another, she was most likely to appear in the records of her owner, Francis Sorrel: his business papers, his slave lists, his bills of sale for human property, his census listings, his personal letters, his ledger or account books, and so on. Matilda Anne Moxley Sorrel was also someone in whose written records Molly might be found. Molly was a domestic slave whose primary duties would have been the care of Matilda and her children, the upkeep of the manor house, and the preparation and service of meals and refreshments. As mistress of this stately home, Matilda would have been the manager of Molly's labor. Matilda would have instructed and reprimanded Molly, over-seen and punished her, and complained about or praised Molly in letters to her friends or relatives back home. Wives of philandering slaveholders, often referred to in African American literature studies as the recurring "jealous mistress" character type, had a tendency to write about black women in personal diaries and letters, even to the point of confessing and bemoaning illicit sexual relations between their husbands and female slaves.[2]

I found that the prominent Sorrel family had left a traceable, though not extensive, set of records. Most of these records were housed in the Georgia Historical Society located not far from the Sorrel home in historic Savannah. Personal letters between the family and close friends pre-served at the National Archives in Washington, D.C., also provided access to the Sorrel family members' lives. So did letters written about promi-nent Savannahians by one of their own, Mayor Charles Jones, which are gathered in the published collection *Children of Pride*. A Civil War mem-oir by Francis and Matilda's most famous son, Confederate brigadier gen-eral Moxley Sorrel, also includes brief memories of his parents' lives.[3]

As it turns out, however, none of the Sorrel family's publicly available records mention a slave named Molly or a relationship between Fran-cis and a female slave or a murder committed in the carriage house. While an interracial sex-suicide-murder scandal like this one is some-thing the family might have worked hard to conceal, it seems likely that dramatic double deaths within a two-week period on the grounds of a high-profile estate would have appeared somewhere in the public record of close-knit Savannah society—in a newspaper story or letter by members of the Sorrel social set or in a memoir or diary of Madison Square residents. Certainly, the untimely death of Matilda Sorrel due to "concussion to the brain" does appear in the historical record.[4]

But there is not a trace of Molly. I found no indication that Francis Sor-rel ever owned a woman named Molly or had a sexual relationship with a slave leading to two deaths. It is possible that I missed something, but I doubt it. It is possible that the current homeowners and ghost-tour guides have secret evidence, but I doubt that too. More likely, most likely, the story was fabricated. When I sought the aid of an archivist at the Georgia Histor-ical Society in solving the mystery of Molly, I received a letter saying this:

I would caution anyone to take what they hear on a tour with a grain of salt unless they also provide the documentation to sustain it. The only mention of an affair between Francis Sorrel and anyone else has been in relation to the ghost tour at the house. I have found no documentation at all mentioning an affair. Matilda Ann D. Sorrel did die from injuries sustained in a fall on March 27, 1860. Her death is not listed as a suicide, and she is buried in Laurel Grove Cemetery in the family plot. . . . There is no mention in any papers or family histories of the subsequent death of anyone connected with the Sorrel family. . . . From all accounts Francis Sorrel was a well-respected man in Savannah with no suspicion on him.

The meaning of the letter was plain. The archivist thought me naive. Perhaps she also sought to protect the reputation of a leading Savannah family from further ignominy, but this did not discount her implicit critique.

And maybe the archivist was right. Maybe I *had* been naive and overly reactive in the aftermath of my intense reaction to the Sorrel-Weed House tours. It turned out that Molly really was a kind of ghost, a figment of human imagination. Although many young women like her surely existed in antebellum Savannah and the torturous rice plantations of the surrounding countryside, this Molly was not among them. Someone had concocted her story of racial and sexual exploitation as a titillating tourist attraction. And now I wanted to know why.

If I could not find Molly, I would search for the reasons *why* she was invisible in the historical record yet hypervisible on the Savannah ghost-tourism scene. And this search led me to a host of other questions. Why were ghost stories about African American slaves becoming popular in the region at all? And why were so many of these ghosts women? What themes prevailed in slave ghost stories, and what social and cultural meanings can we make of them? What "product" was being bought and sold, enjoyed and consumed, in the contemporary commercial phenomenon of southern ghost tourism?

Graveyard Dust and Voodoo Queens: The Making of Spooky Savannah

In Savannah, Georgia, a sleepy city by the sea, tourism surged with the publication of a true-crime tell-all known by locals as "The Book."[5] First published in 1994, *Midnight in the Garden of Good and Evil*, by journalist John Berendt, was a number 1 national bestseller for more than four years.[6] *Midnight* was a combination travelogue and true-crime exposé interwoven with Berendt's first-person story of life in his quaint, adopted town. As a part-time resident of Savannah for over eight years, Berendt came to know the insular city's most colorful personalities. He profiled figures such as the well-heeled antiques collector Jim Williams and transgendered African American nightclub performer Lady Chablis in a suspenseful retelling of a murder investigation and the dramatic courtroom battles that followed. Berendt's account of the 1981 shooting death of young, brash Danny Hansford allegedly at the hands of his lover and employer, the older and sophisticated Jim Williams, combined true crime with the atmospheric setting of the moss-cloaked coastal South. Central to Berendt's characterization of Savannah as a fascinating city stuck in the past was his representation of Voodoo. The title of his book referred to the cemetery, or conjurer's "garden," where African American "witch doctor" and "Voodoo priestess" Minerva assisted Jim Williams in his legal defense through the use of Voodoo rituals. Williams reportedly told Berendt, "Whether you know it or not, you are in the heart of voodoo country. The whole coastal area has been loaded with it since the slaves brought voodoo with them from Africa." Minerva, Williams goes on to explain, was continuing the practice of her "common-law" husband, the locally notorious but by then deceased "root doctor" Dr. Buzzard. Minerva lived in a "wooden shanty" painted "haint blue" to "ward off evil spirits." She appointed midnight as the time for doing magic in the "flower garden" and informed Jim Williams that the spirit of the dead boy was "workin' hard against him."[7] Jim Williams was convicted twice of murder in the 1980s, but the Georgia Supreme Court overturned his convictions for procedural reasons. After judges declared a mistrial in a third go-around due to a hung jury, Williams's fourth trial was moved to a different venue. A jury in Augusta acquitted him of the crime and made him the only person ever to be tried four times for murder in the state of Georgia. Williams attributed his release to Minerva's spiritual interventions, only to die of pneumonia seven months after his acquittal in January 1990.[8] Berendt's book about the legal case and evocative setting put Savannah, a town formerly off the beaten track, on the map of alluring American places. In a *New York Times* review of the book in 1994, Glenna Whitley concluded by writing: "*Midnight in the Garden of Good and Evil* might be the first true-crime book that makes the reader want to call a travel agent and book a bed and breakfast for an extended weekend at the scene of the crime."[9]

The *New York Times* reviewer had put her finger on the pulse of a moment and likely helped to quicken it. Tourists came to town in droves seeking out locations in "The Book," especially when filming began for a feature film based on the story in 1997. Thematic tours focusing on sites in *Midnight in the Garden of Good and Evil* accommodated these desires. Bonaventure Cemetery, featured on the cover of the book and described as the setting for Minerva's final Voodoo ritual, became a must-see attraction. The fame that John Berendt had brought to Savannah was due in no small part to his narrative linkage between the city and Voodoo, or in Minerva's quoted words, "Black magic" that "never stops."[10]

The popularity of *Midnight* spurred tourism and increased the value of homes in the Savannah Historic District, an area encompassing the riverfront and twenty-two eighteenth-century parklike squares that had gained National Historic Landmark status in 1966. The Mercer-Williams House, former home of Jim Williams, was located in the heart of the historic district on lovely Monterey Square. As tourism boomed, attracting 5 million visitors a year by 1999 and becoming a $1 billion industry in the city by 2003, increasing numbers of stately homes were purchased, improved, and sometimes incorporated into tours of historic Savannah.[11] Historic district tours made profitable by the popularity of *Midnight* were soon joined by haunted Savannah tours. Most ghost walking tours, which made up over half of all walking tours taken in Savannah, featured the human drama of city history.[12] According to geographer Glenn Gentry, "As the setting of the popular book and film *Midnight in the Garden of Good and Evil*, Savannah has invested heavily into ghost-tourism development and the use of murder, tragedy, and mystery as marketing tools."[13] Six years after Gentry published his findings, local writer Amy Paige Condon reported on her foray into the booming Savannah ghost-tour subculture for *Savannah Magazine*. She asserted that Savannah's "dark star ascended in 2002" after the city was named Most Haunted by the American Institute of Parapsychology. By the time she made her observations in the spring of 2013, she found that "macabre" was "big business," with more than twenty companies running ghost tours in Savannah as part of the larger dark-tourism industry.[14]

The Midnight Zombie Tour of haunted places that I took along with two dozen other people during my second visit to Savannah on a warm spring evening in 2013 was offered by one of those twenty companies: Blue Orb Tours. The popular Midnight Zombie Tour was a dark parade through Savannah's haunted places that used *Midnight in the Garden of Good and Evil* as a touchstone. Not only did the tour borrow a keyword from Berendt's book title, but it also included a stop at the Mercer-Williams House, where the murder featured in *Midnight* took place. The dynamic tour guide, Tobias McGriff, told our group about the famous crime, emphasizing Jim Williams's wealth and personal collection of evil objects, such as Adolf Hitler's last SS suit and car hood ornament. True to the story line of Berendt's book, McGriff said that in seeking occult help with his murder trial, Williams had consulted the most powerful conjurer in the area: Minerva, widow of the famous Doctor Buzzard and, McGriff added, second cousin to New Orleans "Voodoo Queen" Marie Laveau. But McGriff informed us that Williams was more evil than Minerva herself, who reportedly told him in a quotation that does not appear in the book, "You are darker than I am." McGriff told those on our tour that according to Gullah and Geechee people (the descendants of black slaves in the area), Williams's death was actually due to black magic rather than the natural causes cited by Berendt; Minerva had "dusted" Williams (or killed him with a toxic dust) because of a falling out between the pair resulting from Williams's consultation with a Latina Santeria practitioner. McGriff emphasized that New Orleans is not the only place with a history of Voodoo; Voodoo was flourishing right there in Savannah, Georgia. McGriff's provocative assertion echoed Jim Williams's claim that had been captured and popularized in *Midnight in the Garden of Good and Evil*: that Savannah was a hot spot for Voodoo due to the lingering practices of the descendants of slaves.

Ghost Land: Southern Space and the National Imagination

Within a decade of the publication of "The Book," Savannah had become an epicenter of the ghost-touring zeitgeist. In 2002 the American Institute of Parapsychology, a Florida-based research center dedicated to supernatural studies, awarded Savannah the title of America's Most Haunted City. Savannah trumped other predictably haunted places like Salem, Massachusetts, associated with the eighteenth-century Salem witch trials (which actually happened in present-day Danvers, one town over); Gettysburg, Pennsylvania, location of the bloody Civil War battle; and New Orleans, Louisiana, home of the infamous Voodoo "priestess" Marie Laveau, to become the ultimate ghost hunting hub. The institute's director, Dr. Andrew Nichols, told me why Savannah had come out on top for the Most Haunted award, a singular, all-time honor. He wrote in response to my emailed query,

> The American Institute of Parapsychology awarded the honorary designation of "American's Most Haunted City" to Savannah in 2002, in conjunction with our conference held in that beautiful city. We based our award (and the selection of this site for our conference) on the fact that we had received more reports of haunting-type activity from Savannah during the previous five years than from any other American city. Other contenders for the title were New Orleans, Charleston SC, and St. Augustine FL. All the old colonial cities have a higher probability factor for hauntings due to the abundance of ancient structures, which have remained relatively unchanged since early times.[15]

I realized, upon reading Dr. Nichols's explanation, that all of the major contenders for the Most Haunted award had been southern cities. Why, I wondered, would the South be privileged when it comes to designating haunted American places? Dr. Nichols emphasized the colonial history of each town, and yet Salem, Massachusetts, did not make his list, although Salem is older than Savannah by more than 100 years. It seems that even Puritan villages famous for witchcraft cannot compete with the South for specters. Neither, apparently, can a region like Washington Irving's Hudson River Valley, a storied place rife with past and present hauntings.[16] There was something more at work in Nichols's list than immediately met the eye. The reason for singling out the South as America's haunted hot spot was not solely its age, I thought, but also its history of chattel slavery and the brutal war to end it, both set against a foreboding backdrop of swamps, woods, thickets, and mist. According to popular lore and common knowledge alike, ghosts dwell in places stained by unresolved conflict—places marked by pain, violence, betrayal, suffering, and ugly death. The enslavement of millions of African Americans and tens of thousands of Native Americans between 1529 (Hernando de Soto's expedition through the Southeast) and 1866 is an original sin in America's founding, and the cataclysmic Civil War that resulted is a conflict seared into the flesh of the culture.[17]

Certainly slavery occurred across all the colonies, states, and territories of the United States in various forms and with various victims (Native American concubines to fur trade merchants in Detroit, unfree Chinese prostitutes and railway laborers in California, black enslaved miners in southern Illinois, and on and on). But the South is the only region in the nation where extensive, elaborate plantation culture thrived for over two centuries; where slaves became stage props for their owners' neo-aristocratic lifestyles; and where slaveholders as a class banded together to wage a war to retain human property. Restaurateur and media personality Paula Deen's recent admission that she dreamed of planning a "traditional" southern wedding with African American waiters dressed up as slaves captures the cultural history of spectacular oppression that I am pointing to. (Deen owns a famous southern food restaurant in Savannah. I was advised by locals to go to Mrs. Wilkes's instead.)[18] In short, the South has made a habit, a cause, and even a spectacle of human bondage. The history of race-based dehumanization and exploitation, and the doggedness with which southern leaders defended slavery to the point of sacrificing 300,000 lives in the Civil War, has made the South a site of unhealed social wounding, a psychic repository of unresolved conflict, a symbolic space of remembered wrongs in our national consciousness. And even as the South is haunted by slavery, America is haunted by the slaveholding South.

Here is what Margaret Wayt DeBolt, popular author of *Savannah Spectres*, writes about why the South is so haunted: "Are there really ghosts in the South? . . . You bet your sweet magnolia there are! The antebellum South isn't dead—it's merely wandering, rising, hovering and drifting from plantation to plantation, searching for lost loves and old enemies."[19] The cover of DeBolt's 1984 book, which launched the city's ghost book trend, features the main house of Coldbrook Plantation set in a shrunken landscape of withered grass and craggy shrubs. The wood house hunkers in a state of moody disrepair with dingy white siding, dilapidated roofing, and broken windowpanes with half-gone shutters. This image of a recalcitrant South decayed by loss and corruption is the essence of the southern gothic form of American literature perfected by authors William Faulkner and Flannery O'Connor. Faulkner's famous quotation "The past is never dead. It's not even past" is reflected in DeBolt's comments about the undead antebellum South and sets the tone for place-based haunting stories.[20]

Every region of this nation has ghost stories, but the South *feels* more haunted than the rest. Due to its brutal history of indigenous land theft and "removal," of black chattel bondage and racialized torture, and of ugly civil war, the southern soil is soaked with unquiet blood. The geographic boundary of this slaveholding space symbolizes Americans' deepest national shame, a conjoined trauma of dispossession and dehumanization to which we must return in order to understand ourselves and make peace with one another. The South, therefore, functions like a storehouse for the nation's historical guilt, a sociocultural archive accessed through stories of haunting. This explains why southern ghosts of slavery remain with us even now, calling us to confront them. The ways in which we imagine, narrativize, and contend with these ghosts seems paramount, then, to the public history discussion of how we remember slavery.[21]

The Most Haunted House in Savannah

It was in the immediate afterglow of the publication of *Midnight in the Garden of Good and Evil* that Stephen Bader and his brother, Philip Bader, purchased the "Old Sorrel-Weed House," an impressive mansion built by well-known architect Charles B. Cluskey on the northern edge of Madison Square in the mid-1800s. Stephen Bader had been employed as an investment banker in Atlanta when his brother told him to be on the lookout for a historic home to purchase. The pair paid $645,000 for the property in 1996, acquiring it through a limited liability corporation called Sorrel Weed Restorations. Stephen Bader told reporters that he descended from Robert E. Lee, a visitor to the Sorrel-Weed home during the Civil War, and proclaimed a love for history as his motivation for buying the property. He began to restore the house, though not without contention from the Historic Review Board, the Occupational Safety and Health Administration, and neighbors. Bader was criticized for hiring laborers off the street who had no training in historic restoration, for making shoddy repairs, for worsening the building's cracked and sinking foundation, and for painting the home a pumpkin-orange color that some onlookers found offensive. A neighbor who was suing Bader over damages allegedly caused by his construction work charged him with having a "California Gold Rush . . . mentality" and lamented, "that poor house, that pooooor house!" The Bader brothers also encountered financial setbacks, which led at one point to the attempted repossession of several antique furniture pieces that Stephen Bader had selected for the renovation. According to media reports, he was ultimately unable to afford his plan to redecorate the home in 1840s period style.[22]

Soon after Savannah's ascendance as a Most Haunted place, Stephen Bader began to tell stories about ghosts on the premises that he said had been active during restoration efforts. A construction worker employed by Bader who was living in the carriage house also reported that he had heard a voice whispering in the night and had seen evidence of furniture having been mysteriously rearranged.[23] After 2003, Bader opened the Sorrel-Weed House for public ghost tours. When I visited the home a decade later, the tour script included the admission that restoration of the building was still under way. Based on the stories of Sorrel-Weed owners as well as site staff that were soon embellished by local tour companies and visitors to the home, the Sorrel-Weed House was by then officially haunted. The home was so well known for its ghosts after years of recirculated stories and visitors posting images online at the website www.sorrelweedhouse.com/ghostpictures that it had become a regular stop on ghost tours. Tour companies that did not have a special arrangement to take their customers inside the building still stopped in Madison Square beyond the home's gates. Writer Amy Paige Condon reported that her guide on the Haunted Savannah Tour halted at the home and used his iPad to play the audio of "a servant woman's screams as she's being hung at the Sorrel Weed House."[24] That "servant woman" was Molly, the black enslaved girl whose story had so disturbed me on my first trip to Savannah. Molly's screams, supposedly caught on tape by the *Ghost Hunters* television show, are reposted widely on YouTube and hence made available to tour guides and vanloads of tourists.

The haunting phenomenon at the Sorrel-Weed House, while perhaps very real to believers who visit, might also be seen as an ingenious financial strategy for holding on to this costly architectural gem. In a high-profile, high-traffic historic district, the owners of Sorrel-Weed could market tickets for tours of a home that was never fully restored, a home that possessed an aura of gloom due to its state of disrepair. By inserting a degree of creativity and relying on the expectations of tourists, there was potential to profit from a damaged house by highlighting its resident ghosts. In the case of Sorrel-Weed, *not* restoring a historic site to its former glory became the ticket to economic viability. The homeowners could protect their investment in real time by fabricating a story about human property in past time. Like *Midnight in the Garden of Good and Evil*, the "most haunted house in Savannah," as the Sorrel-Weed House was soon dubbed, highlighted black characters and black spirituality for popular appeal. For the homeowners as well as for the ghost-tour companies that incorporate the Sorrel-Weed House, the

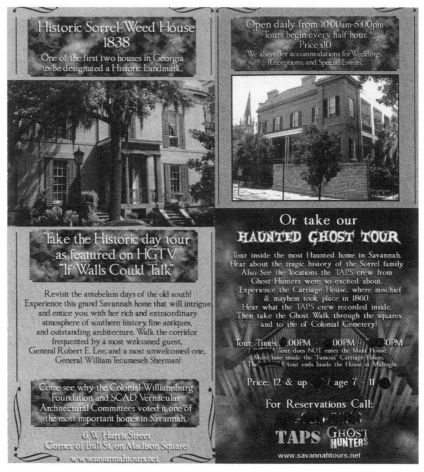

Sorrel-Weed House brochure. This brochure was collected by the author at the Sorrel-Weed House in Savannah in 2012. Advertised tours at the site included the "historic" day tour and evening ghost or paranormal tours.

interlinked deaths of Molly and Matilda, and the hauntings that followed, were golden opportunities.

The ghost story hinges on the gory deaths of two women, one black and one white, in the 1860s and on the Haitian background of the home's original French owner, cotton merchant Francis Sorrel. Francis Sorrel's affair with a slave girl named Molly, discovered by his wife Matilda, led to the demise of both women—Matilda by suicide and Molly by murder. Their ghosts are said to haunt "Shady Corner," the fondly named Sorrel family home at 6 West Harris Street, and have been seen, heard, and otherwise sensed by multiple visitors.[25] Creator of the Midnight Zombie

Tour, Tobias McGriff, devotes a chapter to the Sorrel-Weed House in his book, *Savannah Shadows*. "This Greek Revival masterpiece created a perfect storm for one of the most haunted residences in the country," McGriff writes before recounting the story of the tragic trio and describing a visit to the Sorrel-Weed House with psychic Jenny Wright. McGriff recounts that during this evening visit, he urged the Sorrel-Weed night manager to "take us straight to the money shots . . . the room where Matilda jumped and the carriage house where Molly was found hanged." McGriff reports nothing of paranormal interest in Matilda's room. But in Molly's room, the psychic who accompanied McGriff sensed a presence. Standing beside the window "prayerfully, with her fingers interlocked," the psychic asked the spirits, "Is there anything you would like to say. . . . Is anyone here?" Through the thermal meter that McGriff was using to monitor temperature fluctuations in the room, he saw a "slender, undeniably human form" take shape just as the psychic whispered, "Someone is here." According to McGriff, that night they had encountered the "Haitian slave girl named Molly," who was "in her early twenties and quite beautiful."[26]

McGriff describes Molly and her "affair" with the "shipping magnate" in language that could grace the back cover of a bodice-ripper historical romance. The four times that I took the Sorrel-Weed House tour between 2012 and 2013, I noted similarly romanticized portrayals of Molly and her predicament. Molly's sexual relationship with Francis Sorrel was presented as consensual by various tour guides, who emphasized a narrative of choice by referring to Molly as Sorrel's "mistress" and calling their relationship an "affair." Only once did I hear a tour guide express sensitivity and a critical awareness of Molly's subjugated position. That guide, a young African American woman with a quiet demeanor and natural hairstyle, inserted a brief comment at the end of her script about the sexual connection between Francis and Molly. "It's sad," she told our group of eight on a warm weekday in late spring. "Whether Molly had said yes or no, it would have been the same outcome." This single tour guide's insightful commentary notwithstanding, Molly's situation in the Sorrel-Weed House haunting story is often presented as a free choice. But in contrast to this distorted version of events, during the slavery era numerous white men took advantage of their total authority over black women's bodies to force, coerce, or cajole sexual contact.[27]

The unsavory Sorrel-Weed ghost story ties Molly's fate to the documented death of Matilda Sorrel, Francis's second wife. Matilda Ann

Douglass Moxley married Francis Sorrel in 1829 after the death of her sister, Lucinda Ireland Moxley, Francis's first wife. Francis and Lucinda had three children. Francis and Matilda had five children, including Alexander Claxton Sorrel, who would serve as a major in the Confederate army, and Gilbert Moxley Sorrel, who would become a Confederate brigadier general and memoirist of the Civil War.[28] Little has been written about Matilda, a devout Presbyterian who was described by a member of her social set as "subject to great mental depressions."[29] Matilda died prematurely at age fifty-four on March 27, 1860.[30] According to Charles Jones, mayor of Savannah, on that day Matilda "sprang probably in a fit of lunacy . . . from the second or third story window of her residence on Harris Street, next door to the house which was the family mansion for so many years."[31] Matilda did fall to her death as the ghost story describes, though apparently not at the Sorrel-Weed historic home. She died at 12 West Harris Street, the townhouse next door that Sorrel had purchased for the family in 1859.[32] While two of her peers felt that Matilda's demise was psychologically induced, the death record does not indicate suicide and only cites "concussion" as the cause.

The provocative pairing of Molly the slave and Matilda the mistress at the core of a tale of sexual jealousy and domestic strife indicates the extent to which tourism professionals and visitors to southern sites are aware of the tumultuous sexual dynamics of the antebellum era. Yet how this story is told trivializes that latent consciousness. Firsthand accounts by black enslaved women and white women slaveholders alike articulate the southern horror only alluded to in the Sorrel-Weed ghost tour: the destruction of black lives as well as white families by the unfettered beast of sexual slavery. Domestic tranquility proved to be elusive, and indeed, impossible, in the South's most elegant homes. Tourists of the American South suspect this horror and even seek to safely confront it, which is perhaps what makes Sorrel-Weed the most infamous historic home in present-day Savannah.

International Man of Mystery: A Portrait of Francis Sorrel

While the embellished death of Matilda and imagined death of Molly anchor the Sorrel-Weed hauntings, it is really the patriarch of the home, Francis Sorrel himself, who dominates this story. The tour script at the Sorrel-Weed House describes Sorrel as an emigrant from Haiti who appears to be white but is secretly black. Through this deception, he leads an upstanding white family to give him not one but two daughters in marriage. He is a practitioner of the occult Voodoo religion who betrays his wedding vows and drives his Christian wife to suicide. He is the likely murderer of his enslaved young lover, but he is never punished for this or any other crime. Instead, Sorrel lives an abnormally long life, possibly due to his practice of ritualistic "black" magic.

Francis Sorrel's villainy would not be so complete, nor nearly so acceptable, if he were an authentic white patriarch in this story. It is his hidden blackness—his hidden black foreignness—that propels and explains his terrible chain of transgressions. More dangerous than an identifiable black man who does bad things within the limits of segregated black society, Francis Sorrel appears white enough to infiltrate Savannah's upper crust but maintains his subjective allegiance to blackness in the story. He hails from the country most associated with Voodoo. He is described as a carefree master who barely works his slaves. He takes a black Haitian woman for his lover. He carries out mysterious rites that may include human sacrifice. He was even alive and present during the Haitian Revolution, the ultimate historical symbol of black rebellion.[33] It is more than possible that Francis Sorrel's "true" character as a black man passing for white in this story taps into barely submerged anxieties in modern-day America about racial integration, black masculinity, and the criminality associated with black men. But was Francis Sorrel really a free man of color who harbored hidden allegiances to Afro-Haitian cultural ways? The answer to this question is elusive. While piecing together the main events of Francis Sorrel's life is possible through family letters and biographical sketches, census records, and newspaper articles, proof of his racial ancestry remains obscure. Existing sources reveal a man who faced early trauma, built great wealth, and drew on racial privilege at the expense of others.

Francois (Francis) Sorrel was born on the Mirigoane Plantation in St. Domingue on May 4, 1793. His father was the French military colonel Antoine Sorrel. His mother was the colonel's second wife, Eugénie de Sutre, who died the month after Francis's birth.[34] Antoine Sorrel had inherited the plantation from his first wife and owned several slaves in Haiti. Family histories contend that Francis Sorrel was separated from his family during black assaults on white plantations in the Haitian Revolution of 1791–1804. Cut off from his father, Francis grew up with his deceased mother's relatives on the coast in Port au Prince, where he became an accountant and administrative secretary in the firm of brothers Richard and George Douglass. In 1812 Francis transferred with the company to Baltimore; in 1818 he transferred again to Savannah. Soon he and Richard Douglass cofounded the new firm Douglass and Sorrel in Savannah, which advertised consumable goods for sale. In 1822 Francis married into his business partner's family, the Douglasses and the Moxleys, slaveholders from Virginia who maintained a plantation there as well as their home in Baltimore. By 1826 Francis Sorrel owned three black slaves. In 1827–28 he helped his cousin and aging father, who had also immigrated to America and settled with relatives in Louisiana, to acquire slaves.[35]

Francis married Moxley women twice in the 1820s, first Lucinda, and then her younger sister, Matilda, while expanding his scope of influence in Savannah at a time when the city was beginning to boom as a result of the cotton crop. After 1800, inland planters in the region had turned away from rice, indigo, and sea island cotton and toward short-staple cotton, a favorite of European industrial buyers. The efficient processing of cotton made possible by the technological innovation of the cotton gin meant the crop could be produced and sold in large quantities. As an ambitious, experienced merchant and shipper in what would become one of the nation's three largest port cities in the 1850s, Francis Sorrel was well positioned for economic success.[36] His profits rose in the antebellum cotton boomtown of Savannah. He purchased stock in pivotal companies, such as the Central Georgia Railroad, which was key to the transportation of cotton from outlying Georgia and South Carolina plantations to the Savannah port. He established the Francis Sorrel Company and built a massive office complex near the riverfront across from the Customs House. A practicing Presbyterian, he held a number of influential business and civic posts, including serving as the long-time director of the Planters Bank.[37] By 1840 Sorrel had his showpiece Greek Revival mansion designed and built on Madison Square.[38] By 1850 he had five slaves on the premises and served as the "trustee" for eight "mulatto" slaves, ages three to thirty-five. The individuals listed as his wards were likely slaves who worked in the city but were owned by whites outside the city and answered to Sorrel as a guardian in the absence of their owners. In Savannah and other southern port cities, urban slavery and rural slavery were inextricably linked, such that plantation owners had regular business in town and put their slaves to work in either location. According to the slave schedule in Georgia's census for the year 1860, sixty-seven-year-old Francis Sorrel had in his possession eight slaves at that time. One of these was a twenty-year-old female designated as "mulatto." She is not named in the record.[39] Although there is no evidence that the figure called Molly actually existed, it is not beyond the realm of possibility that Sorrel, like many other southern patriarchs, was involved with a slave woman during his lifetime. In 1859, nearly two decades after building his corner-lot mansion, Sorrel sold the place to Henry Weed and moved his family next door to a stylish Victorian townhome. One year later, in 1860, Sorrel's wife Matilda died suddenly, falling from an upper window of the townhome and planting the seed for the twenty-first-century ghost story.

No apparent primary evidence indicates that Francis Sorrel had African ancestry. However, local historian Carla Weeks suggests this was possible, and she cites intriguing reasons. She bases her conclusion mainly on the circumstantial evidence that Francis's father, Antoine, abandoned him as a child and omitted him from the will while maintaining ties with the children of a former marriage. Weeks also says that a family history written by one of the descendants and held privately by a descendant today shows that successive generations of the Sorrel family did not discuss Francis's mother, Eugénie de Sutre. Given the absence of his mother in an otherwise detailed family history, Weeks suggests that de Sutre may have indeed been a free woman of color.[40]

If Francis Sorrel *were* a free man of color in possession of slaves in antebellum Savannah, he would not have been alone. The free black population in Savannah had decreased since the eighteenth century as a result of the adoption of stricter manumission laws in 1801 and 1818, but in 1840 there were still 632 free blacks in Savannah; in the late 1850s there were 705.[41] A fair number among this group had been emigrants from St. Domingue in the wake of the Haitian Revolution, a pattern to which Francis's biography coheres.[42] White political leaders in Savannah sought to control this free black population by passing an antiblack code in 1818 that required annual registration, compelled free blacks to commit thirty hours of unpaid labor to the city, and denied free blacks the right to buy land. In the 1830s and '40s, restrictions on free blacks contracted still further. Despite numerous legal limitations on their personal freedoms, free people of color could possess black slaves, though they could not purchase new slaves after that ability was restricted in 1818. Most often, free blacks owned members of their own families or friends whom they had purchased to help those individuals achieve greater autonomy. Some slaveholding people of color engaged in the practice of slaveholding to benefit economically from slave labor, but this group was in the minority.[43] Francis Sorrel only knew the scent and touch of his mother for six weeks before her death during his infancy. He would not have remembered her, but he did grow up in the care of her relatives as a young child. If Sorrel was passing for white in an American context but recognized his mother's family as free people of color with whom he identified, perhaps he made an active decision to aid other mixed-race people by signing on as their "trustees" in the census and owning them as slaves whom he treated with relative permissiveness.

It is interesting indeed to reimagine Francis Sorrel's biography within the categorical frame of a free person of color; however, no concrete evidence demonstrates that he was either a man of color or particularly thoughtful toward his slaves. The documentary record indicates instead that Sorrel was what he appeared to be: a wealthy white Christian slaveholder. Certainly Sorrel's children revealed no awareness of African ancestry or empathy with the black freedom struggle. Francis Sorrel's mother's ancestry remains a mystery—one that the contemporary owners of his home are able to use to their advantage in promoting him as an exotic black man in disguise.[44]

The preservation of the Sorrel-Weed House as a historic site that is open to the public holds in memory a cache of potent, painful stories. In very few other places on the tourist circuit in Savannah are visitors presented with the shadow of slavery in so blatant a form. Although Molly in the Sorrel-Weed tale seems not to have been a real person, many young women with stories like Molly's populated the slave quarters and surrounding plantations of antebellum Savannah. When interpreted critically and not romantically, as the Sorrel-Weed tour script would have it, Molly's ghostly presence marks the spot where actual African American women in slavery struggled with untold sexual abuse. The mystery surrounding Francis Sorrel's background is likewise telling in how it opens questions about interracial sex, mixed-race heritage, and complex allegiances in southern elite identities. And what is more, discussions of Francis's history in his children's papers reveal the dark, psychologically consuming horror that members of the slaveholding class harbored: not a fear of ghosts, but a fear of black rebellion. Francis Sorrel's daughter Aminta captured this terror in her paper on her father's life, where she wrote the following: "Francis Sorrel was about four or five years old when the Insurrection took place, and at the time of the terrible massacre and terrible deeds of the infuriated natives. . . . He remembered

OLD SORREL—WEED HOUSE

A fine example of Greek Revival style, this building (completed in 1840 from the plans of Charles B. Cluskey, a well-known Georgia architect) shows the distinguished trend of Savannah architecture during the first half of the 19th century. The Mediterranean villa influence reflects the French background of the original owner, Francis Sorrel (1793-1870), a shipping merchant of Savannah who as a child was saved by a faithful slave from the massacre of the white colonists in St. Domingo. The ante-bellum tradition of refinement and hospitality associated with the residence was continued after its purchase in 1859 by Henry D. Weed.

Here resided as a youth G. Moxley Sorrel (1838-1901) who achieved fame as one of "Lee's Lieutenants." Shortly after war broke out in 1861 Sorrel, a young bank clerk in Savannah, proceeded to Virginia where he obtained a place on Gen. Longstreet's staff. He served with conspicuous valor and zeal through the major battles and campaigns in that theater from the First Manassas to Petersburg and was thrice wounded. Sorrel became brig. general at the age of 26. Competent critics have called him "the best staff officer in the Confederate service." Gen. Sorrel's "Recollections of a Confederate Staff Officer" is an absorbing account of his war experiences.

025-27   GEORGIA   HISTORICAL   COMMISSION   1954

Georgia State Historic Site sign, Old Sorrel-Weed House. This Georgia State Historic Site sign for the Old Sorrel-Weed House says the patriarch of the home, Francis Sorrel, was saved by a "faithful slave" in St. Domingue during the Haitian Revolution. Photo by the author, 2013.

the fearful scenes he witnessed, little children torn asunder and cut into pieces, and the savage and wholesale butchery made such an impression upon him, that whenever narrating the events to his children, he would become very nervous and tremble with excitement."[45] Francis's son Moxley echoed his sister's recollections, writing about their father, "He was a child witness of many bloody scenes and deeds of hideous atrocity perpetrated by the blacks. They long haunted his memories. Recalling them even in his old age appeared to afflict him with shuddering excitement and we had to restrain our questions."[46] These vivid descriptions of Francis Sorrel's own haunted memories suggest that if Sorrel were to return to tell a story of race and trauma in the parlor of his Greek Revival home today, he would narrate the Haitian Revolution. The historic, bloody struggle in which slaves rose against their French owners to claim their rights as human beings symbolized a constant threat for those who held blacks in bondage, representing the fear that human property would rebel and claim an eye for an eye.

Racial terror, slave rebellion, gendered subjection, sexual abuse: all of these strands of Savannah history, southern history, and slavery history are buried in the Sorrel-Weed ghost story. But it took me several months to unearth them, to dust off the grit of creative marketing, and to peer at the raw entrails underneath. I have a job that allows me to indulge in such scrutiny, not to mention the aid of a wonderful research assistant.[47] How many of the thousands of people who have walked the Sorrel-Weed's darkened halls or listened to Molly's screams on the Internet have the chance to do the same?

The Blue Orb: A Reflection on Savannah's Ghosts

One and a half years after that first trip to Savannah when I felt the call to find Molly the slave girl, I dragged my husband, an academic psychologist, back to the city with me. I wanted to reexperience the Sorrel-Weed House tours, and I wanted to take the Midnight Zombie Tour led by popular paranormal author and radio host Tobias McGriff. I had already read McGriff's book, *Savannah Shadows: Tales from the Midnight Zombie Tour*, which romped gaily through stories of African slave graveyards, Voodoo bone collection, child murder, and deadly hags. McGriff had written that his vision of a marriage "between Colonial Savannah and Conjuring Savannah" and his "experiences in Haiti and Jamaica, as well as the Savannah low country," were what led to his creation of the Blue Orb Tour Company. Savannah was, in McGriff's words, "the holy Mecca for paranormal enthusiasts," and tour guides were "the paranormal priests," operating the "roving confessional of walking ghost tours" and "preach[ing] the ghostly gospel."[48]

African American cultural practices and the history of slavery appear as prominent features of McGriff's book. He devotes a chapter to Voodoo and comments on Obeah, Hoodoo, Voodoo, and black slave ghosts, including Molly of Sorrel-Weed House fame, throughout. He quotes sayings from "Negro" folklore and includes numerous photographs of African-influenced spiritual life: spirit altars and dangling bones, Yoruba village signs, and black cats prowling against the backdrop of African masks. On the inside front flap of his book, a digital imprint can be scanned to open a link showing a Voodoo possession ritual. (I will never know what this link reveals because I thought better of opening it.) Even the title of the book has black cultural echoes, as the idea of zombies in American popular culture derives from Haitian folklore and scenes of plantation slavery. A zombie is, after all, a slavelike figure whose existence of void consciousness is one of walking death.[49] The first zombie film, *White Zombie* (1932), turned on Voodoo spirit possession among black slaves in Haiti. A white male witch doctor, played by Bela Lugosi in the film, uses the slaves' own ritual to turn them into automaton plantation workers, then casts his spell on a white woman in order to make her his conjugal slave. The themes from this film of forced black labor, black spiritual practice, and white financial interests all have uncanny echoes in McGriff's 2012 book.

In short, I was curious about the author, his tour, and what more I might learn about slave ghosts and dark tourism in Savannah. So late on a Friday evening my husband and I stood among thirty people gathered in Chippewa Square to brave Tobias McGriff's Midnight Zombie Tour. It was Memorial Day weekend, and the spring air hung softly around the group, which was mostly made up of young white women and men, with two Asian men, my husband (who is Native American), and me being the only apparent patrons of color. We had each paid $35 per ticket, and it did not take long to see how McGriff could command such steep fees. He was a showman, a storyteller extraordinaire with an easy, comfortable charisma. He had the look of a vintage magician, a carnival man of bygone days. He was probably in his thirties, with short brown hair. He wore a three-piece black suit over a simple white T-shirt that appeared almost, but not quite, costume like. His opening comment to the group was "I'm a believer." He said he knew everyone present was not a believer like him, that some had been dragged along "by their sweeties in exchange for seeing the *Iron Man 3* movie." Believer or not, McGriff said, he just asked that everyone keep an open mind and have fun. Despite my skeptical view of his book, he had me hooked within moments. Even my ultrarational husband, who most definitely fell within the "dragged along" camp, was pulled into McGriff's web of macabre tales. The dark sky, warm air, and bright moon above infused the evening with a spellbinding feeling of possibility. It was as though we were adults caught up in the childhood pleasure of listening to bedtime stories. And as I would later read in another Savannah tour guide's book, *Savannah Hauntings* by Robert Edgerly, the ghost story claims a closeness to oral storytelling traditions that other contemporary narrative experiences lack.[50] The effect of the crowd, the tales, and the shadows was nothing short of enthralling.

McGriff set off at a brisk pace on the undead streets of late-night Savannah. He led us on foot from Chippewa Square to Colonial Square, Calhoun Square, and Montgomery Square, all the while spinning stories. As we circled around him at the gates of historic Colonial Cemetery, he told us why Savannah had been named the most haunted city in the country. He bragged that Savannah had "beat out" New Orleans, Charleston, Salem, and Gettysburg (which he thought would surely win) because of the many tragic deaths that had occurred here from wars and yellow fever epidemics. People were buried all over the city of Savannah, he said, around 10,000 to 30,000 bodies, and every step of his Savannah walking tour took place over these unmarked graves. Candle Hospital had illegally buried people during the 1820 yellow fever epidemic; some were even buried alive, he reported. Children who were not killed by yellow fever immediately were orphaned by the illness, sickened later, and then were buried separately from loved ones. These orphan children haunted the cemetery as forlorn ghosts. A fifteen-year-old tourist in the city had even caught one child ghost on camera. The video, which McGriff described, featured a shadowy youngster scampering alone around the graves. The ghost bounded up into a tree, hung there like a monkey, then jumped down and leapt across the cemetery before disappearing into a crypt. Our group stood outside the locked cemetery gates, listening to McGriff speak and imagining the motions of the ghost child. Inside the cemetery gates just ahead of us a lantern flickered off and then on again. Members of the group gasped, wondering if this was a ghostly sign. Someone pointed out a black cat crossing from the cemetery into a playground just beyond the gates, a playground where dead children frolicked, McGriff intoned, adding to the palpable mood of suspense.

Along our route of uneven brick paths and narrow side streets, McGriff explained that Savannah had enough Voodoo history to rival New Orleans. He described a Yoruba Voodoo village fifty miles outside of town that had declared itself an independent nation, and he noted that a mixture of Voodoo and Catholicism had long been practiced in Savannah. We soon arrived at Calhoun Square, which McGriff said was a powerful place due to its former use as a slave burial ground. He encouraged us to take photographs, as visitors from the spectral realm had been captured in this spot on previous tours. The area had once been called "weeping square," McGriff told us, "because of what happened here." He said the site had served as an overflow slave pen, where families were sold away from one another and dead slaves were buried callously in shallow, unmarked graves. Unlike other squares, Calhoun was not embellished with fountains and monuments to famous people. "They can't dig far enough down," McGriff explained. "Because of the bodies." He passed around a newspaper clipping describing an incident in which the electric company stopped work here because they had unearthed skeletal remains.

Houses around Calhoun Square were situated on top of the burial ground, McGriff said, and as a result two homes in particular were marked by tragedy and hauntings. We walked to each haunted house, bathed in shadow in the quiet square, and stood beneath the eaves while our tour guide narrated. The ghost of a man who accidentally caused the death of his beloved granddaughter haunted the Epps House. A former Confederate general's shade haunted the house at 432 Abercorn Street, one of the most infamous in Savannah. McGriff said the general had gotten rich on slave-grown cotton and then built a mansion on top of slave graves. On one fateful day, the callous general punished his daughter by tying her to a chair beside a second-floor window in the sweltering summer weather; she died of heat stroke and dehydration and came to haunt the home. The house was now owned by a former member of the Clinton administration but had not been lived in for forty years. McGriff had tried to buy it, he told us, but the owner would not sell because of her religious views and her fear that the home would be turned into a haunted bed-and-breakfast.

McGriff showed us grainy photographs of the ghostly girl in the window, the general's daughter, which had been taken by a tourist. Then he returned our attention to the subject of Voodoo. He cautioned us that "bone collectors" were real and often crept into Calhoun Square to dig up bodies for their Voodoo rituals. He had observed these rituals himself and had digitized one in his book, which he was giving to us as a free gift for taking the tour. As we began to walk again, I fell in beside McGriff. Privately, I asked him if he felt a little on edge, talking about the collection of bones and witnessing "occult" rituals as an outsider. He told me he is a "seeker," that he is sometimes afraid in his work, but fear does not stop him. He seemed serious about this, intense and honest. I believed that he believed what he was telling me.

It was 2:20 A.M. by the time my husband and I finally made it back to our hotel on the edge of Forsythe Park. We were behaving unlike ourselves, like people possessed. We huddled in our room in the renovated Victorian building called The Mansion that serviced Savannah's robust tourism trade. My husband and I were dead tired, but we could not fall asleep. We were exhausted and overstimulated from the Zombie Tour that had not included any zombies.[51] Instead of relaxing, an impossible feat, we reviewed and debated the truth claims of the tour. We searched online and found the video taped by the fifteen-year-old tourist McGriff had mentioned, which had been paired with other videos debunking the existence of the ghost child. The image was grainy, but we could see with our own eyes that the visual evidence did not support our tour guide's story. We felt deflated—not because we wanted the ghost child to be real, or ever thought that it could be, but because we wanted our guide to be real, to have faithfully related what he himself had seen. Next, we fact-checked another of McGriff's stories, using the techno tools of Google and an iPad. We searched for the house at 432 Abercorn Street, so infamous for its spooky aura that tourists sit in Calhoun Square just to gaze at it, and found photographs, videos, and commentaries about the house everywhere online. The owner of the home was never a Confederate general, it seemed, and all of his daughters had died of old age. It felt like our intoxicating midnight tour had been a sham, full of half-truths and cherry-picked details. And worse, it had been a sham shot through with the tragic drama of African American history. Slave pens, Voodoo practitioners, Confederate generals, and cotton fields all added to the allure of the evening's grim tales.

Later, back home in Michigan, I typed up my handwritten notes and uploaded my photographs from the historic sites my husband and I had visited during the trip: the Sorrel-Weed House, Wormsloe Plantation, the Mercer House, and more. I gasped when I saw something floating in the middle of an image: a bright blue orb. In one of my pictures of Calhoun Square, the so-called slave burial ground from the Midnight Zombie Tour, a blue-tinted sphere hovered above the ground. Two other spheres glowing white floated in the darkness around it. These were orbs, so-called digital imprints of spirits that are invisible to the naked eye. Blue- and purple-colored orbs are reportedly the most powerful, the most spirit-laden. I could not believe what I was seeing. I called my husband in to view the picture, seeking corroboration or a rational explanation; I did not quite know which. My four-year-old son burst into the room behind my husband, lured by the intrigue of parental commotion.

"What's that, Mama, Papa?" he shouted, crowding onto my lap and pointing to the photograph that was open and enlarged on my computer screen. "What's that?" he repeated.

"The grass?" we said, grasping for his meaning, "the field, the light? It's probably just dust. Dust on the camera lens."

"No, not the grass, and not the big blue circle. That thing. That!" After a pause, he sighed. "You don't see it." He held our eyes with the exasperated gaze of an indignant preschooler who knew too much. I looked at my husband. He looked at me. Our son had not only confirmed the presence of the orb, but he had also seen something else besides, something beyond our field of vision and perhaps our understanding. My son's words lingered with me all through that evening, lodging a discomfort that has yet to lift. What if the ghosts of slaves could actually present themselves in old Savannah, conveying messages in digital still life for a modern age? And if spirits could arrest our respectful attention, what would they tell us about their lives? How would they hold us accountable to the difficulties of history? What would they have us do?

2

Madame Lalaurie

French Quarter Fiend

Travelers have long packed a bundle of expectations about what
they will encounter when they visit New Orleans.
—Emily Clark, *The Strange History of the American Quadroon* (2013)

New Orleans is used to spirits. Death is no stranger [to a] legacy of brutality.
—Elizabeth James, Afro-Native professional storyteller (2014)

Gris-Gris Bags and Quadroon Balls:
Touring Supernatural New Orleans

New Orleans, Louisiana, is widely viewed as an intoxicating American
locale, a place characterized by mystery and exotica, rising waters and
Voodoo practitioners, public debauchery, linguistic multiplicity, and
colorful cultural traditions. It is surprising, given the city's mystique that
pulls tourists in like a magnet, that I had lived more than four decades
without ever having visited. My mother, on the other hand, never passes
up a chance to go to New Orleans and says she leaves there feeling both
satisfied and drained. She enjoys the seafood tinged by soul food, the
bold imprint of African American history, and the press of artful people
on the squares, but she feels overcome by what she describes as the
smell of water, briny Mississippi River and salty Atlantic Ocean water
that soaks the streets and atmosphere with a forlorn feeling of loss and
desecration. "Be prepared for the smell," she told me before I left in
January 2013 to see the Crescent City firsthand. And what a jarring experience spending time in New Orleans would turn out to be for a person
in pursuit of the ghosts of slavery.

I had elected, on my second morning in the city, to take a historic
cemetery tour along with several other teachers, professors, and history

practitioners in town for the American Historical Association's annual conference. The winter air was crisp, the sun retiring after a full slate of rain and clouds the day before. Our guide was an earnest white woman in her fifties who took her job of educating the public seriously. With encyclopedic narration at every stop, she hustled our group through three historic cemeteries. Toward the end of our guide's oral survey of the precise engineering and maintenance requirements of shell-encrusted crypts, I asked her whether ghost tours were popular in New Orleans. She told me ghost tours were overly popular in New Orleans, but she would never lead one. "Everybody wants to meet a ghost. I don't," she said.

Our guide had invested instead in studying the concrete histories, architectural features, and physical care of cemeteries. She had earned a certification from the Save Our Cemeteries association and several others, as indicated by the colorful badges and dangling pins attached to the lapel of her denim jacket. She said she preferred to leave the ghost touring to her young adult son who conducted his evening haunted tours by zipping around on a motorized scooter. Our guide's tour was a fitting choice for the studious members of the American Historical Association. But I was willing to bet that her son's evening scooter tour was much more popular. Through a cursory look online, I learned of the overwhelming number of paranormal tours operating in the city, all of them drawing in enough tourist dollars to stay afloat. There were independently run ghost-tour outfits, major tour company offerings, and mom-or-pop ghost tours hosted by enterprising individuals describing themselves as "psychics" or "ordained" Voodoo practitioners. If I wanted to scratch the surface of ghost tourism in New Orleans, I would have to return with more time, and I would have to break away from my fellow historians.

Attending the American Society for Ethnohistory conference made up of historians as well as anthropologists does not seem an auspicious way for me to have enacted the aforementioned plan. But this gathering had the benefit of bringing me back to New Orleans within a year of my first visit and of situating me at the historic and charming Hotel Monteleone, which was within walking distance of numerous ghost-tour sites and, as a bonus feature, was advertised as being haunted.[1] During the day, I attended panels on Native American history. In between conference sessions and especially at night, I donned my dark blue jeans and hit the tourist spots. In hotel lobbies and tour offices around the city, I collected as many brochures for ghost tours as I did for Garden District tours and historic plantation tours. Spirit Tours New Orleans offered ghost, vampire, cemetery, and Voodoo tours daily. NewOrleansGhostTour.com hosted a cemetery tour of "bizarre but true tales" and ghost and vampire tours, with "REAL hauntings" and "REAL history." I could take my pick of this litter. To narrow my choices, I consulted "The Best Haunted Ghost Tours and People to Meet in New Orleans" webpage and tried to select a representative range.[2] I opted for the mainstream Gray Line Tours company's Cemetery and Voodoo Tour, a specialized Haunted History New Orleans Ghost Tour, and an independent tour led by Karen Jeffries, a local psychic and expert in paranormal investigations.

My companion participants on the New Orleans ghost tours were eclectic and fairly heterogeneous, the most diverse groups that I saw anywhere during my travels. They were mostly young to middle aged, from all over the United States and at least one foreign country. They were white, black, Latino, and Asian, dressed in high-fashion silk tanks and worn-out athletic team T-shirts, carrying Louis Vuitton bags and open-lid alcoholic beverages. On the evening tours, it would not be a stretch to say that a third of the participants were drunk or drinking, or that the tour companies encouraged this behavior by scheduling breaks in bars and guaranteeing discounted Hurricane drinks at Pat O'Brien's landmark pub on Bourbon Street.

The Gray Line Cemetery and Voodoo Tour, operated by a sizable mainstream tour company, proved to be the most intellectually stimulating and historically focused of my selections. The ticket cost $25.99 (a discounted online price), and purchasers assembled near the company's riverfront ticket booth to board an air-conditioned bus. The vehicle was full that morning with around twenty riders: one African American (that would be me), two Latinas, one mixed-race black Italian, one white Italian (his mother, it seemed), and several Euro-Americans. Our tour guide (we'll call him Matthew) had a Crocodile-Dundee-in-Greenwich-Village look. He paired a bohemian goatee, long dark ponytail, and wide-brimmed straw hat with cargo pants (water bottle in pocket) and a moisture-resistant techno-fabric T-shirt. He welcomed us, initiated some cheerful banter about people's home cities, then distributed a Gray Line Tour placard along with a small red cotton cloth bundle tied off with black yarn. The gold tag affixed to the bundle read "GRIS-GRIS BAG. Contents: A penny so you will never be poor. Red beans so you will never be hungry. Rice to connect you to mother earth. Bay leaf to spice up your life and enhance your attributes and strengths. Keep this bag with you at all times while in 'The most haunted city in America.' " The back of the tag informed the reader that this magical token was also a coupon that could be presented for "$2.00 off the Ghost & Spirits tour, departing at 7:00 P.M. nightly." I tucked the souvenir Voodoo bag into my tote, wondering what I was in for.

To my surprise, our guide said little about the bag and instead launched into an overview of the city's environmental and social history. Knowledgeable and articulate with an engaging manner, Matthew moved smoothly from ice-age glaciers to French and Spanish colonists to sinking sediment and man-made canals. After hearing our guide's introduction to what we were about to see, we ventured onto the city streets, making our way to St. Louis Cemetery No. 1, the oldest cemetery in the city, which was located on the edge of the black and working-class neighborhood known as Tremé. We entered the high walls of the burial ground and encountered a stone and marble landscape that smelled faintly of urine. Although we had started at 9:00 A.M. that morning, the day was already baking hot. Heat hung over the old stone graves, inten sifying the feeling of enclosure. Members of our group, myself among them, constantly sought shade beneath the walls and rooflines of gothic crypts while taking in our tour guide's arresting narration.

Matthew described New Orleans burial practices in this "city of the dead" and mentioned a number of notable figures, many of them slaveholders, who were interred there. We spent the bulk of our time beside the most famous tomb in the graveyard, belonging (perhaps) to "Voodoo Queen" Marie Laveau. Our guide gave a lengthy talk on the infamous "priestess," explaining that she was actually Catholic, a belief system not incompatible with Voodoo. The powers of mysterious knowledge with which Laveau was credited probably derived from her line of work, he said. She was a hairdresser and seemed to know everyone and their secrets. She sold Voodoo good luck, or "gris-gris" bags much like the ones he had distributed on the bus. Opinions about Laveau were negative in her time and gave Voodoo a bad reputation as malicious. "It isn't," our guide proclaimed, citing people of that faith who practice today.

As we stood beside the tomb that could have been Laveau's (or could have been her daughter's instead; no one knows for sure), Matthew highlighted the offerings that had been left there for her: flowers, trinkets, beads, lipsticks, and hair care products. He explained that the tomb was cleared of these items frequently and whitewashed every few years

Marie Laveau's crypt, New Orleans.
The crypt of Marie Laveau in Historic Cemetery No. 1 in New Orleans
is often decorated by admirers. Photo by the author, 2013.

to erase the graffiti: an XXX sign that visitors often drew on the exterior
walls of the structure, representing a Voodoo ritual that referred, perhaps,
to the Catholic trinity or a West African symbol of physical and spiritual
intersection. Toward the end of the tour Matthew pointed out actor "Nic"
Cage's extra-large pyramidal crypt and noted Cage's past ownership of
the Madame Lalaurie mansion, a famous haunted house in the city. He
also paused at length beside the tomb of Homer Plessy, the early civil
rights activist who protested streetcar segregation in New Orleans, resulting in the famous (and losing) Supreme Court case *Plessy v. Ferguson*.

I was impressed with the Gray Line tour. Our guide covered important material responsibly and managed at the same time to hold the attention of a diverse group. And yet, there was the matter of that gris-gris bag. Matthew had taken pains to carefully explain the biography and religious traditions of Marie Laveau, but the tone of his tour had already been set by a cheap keepsake-cum-coupon that simplified as well as commercialized Voodoo (Vodou or Vodun) beliefs. Afterward, I asked him about his thoughts on ghost tours in New Orleans. Matthew told me the ghost tours were so popular that numerous people, inspired by *Ghost Hunters* and similar shows, came to town just to see ghosts. All the major tour companies have adopted some kind of paranormal tour, he said. And he led those too, because of the demand, though he preferred to do history tours. "But you can still get a lot of history into a ghost tour," Matthew assured me. "Different companies do it in different ways. Some are very theatrical. The way I approach mine is to let my hair down, lighten it up, and have some fun." He was giving a ghost tour that very night and invited me to attend. I couldn't quite imagine this thoughtful man "lightening it up" and wished I could see his rendition of a ghost tour, but I was already booked that evening for a tour with Karen Jeffries, the proprietor of a haunted bed-and-breakfast who was described in my top-ten list as "New Orleans [*sic*] Best and Most Sought After Tour Guide."

Participants in Karen Jeffries's tour assembled at O Bar on Bourbon Street after darkness fell and paid the $20 in cash that she had requested in lieu of advance reservations. Jeffries was not at all what I expected. A woman in her forties or perhaps fifties, she possessed shoulder-length, impossibly wine-red hair and a delicate physical frame. Her playful 1950s-style dress sported a flouncy underskirt and featured a skull print pattern. She carried a skull-and-crossbones purse to match the dress and spoke in a calm, sweet voice. She seemed the opposite of the other tour guides who were visible on the streets that night dressed in dark capes and shouting in booming voices. Her tour had attracted a group of twenty-four people, most of them young and white. Besides me, there was one other black woman in the group, accompanied by an Asian fiancé. There was a woman who appeared to be Filipina with a white husband. There was an actress from Los Angeles with a film coming out soon who was with her new boyfriend but talking incessantly about her old boyfriend. A few of the participants were from New Orleans, including a transgendered woman with her male friend. Three white couples from a small town in North Carolina were taking the tour together. (When a woman in this cluster learned that I was from Michigan during introductions, she informed me that "the South is really haunted" and told me her story of living in a haunted house where a ghost kept turning the thermostat on and off.) I was the only person alone on the tour, as was usually the case with all of the tours I observed. Most people on ghost tours came in pairs or groups and were sociable with their friends as well as strangers. This particular group was chatty and partly drunk. Our guide had encouraged us to grab a drink in the bar if we wished, and many had taken her up on the suggestion.

Karen Jeffries's tour was unusually creative. Rather than focusing on well-known haunted sites and stories, she took guests to sites where she had participated in paranormal investigations. A few of her selections, such as places tied to the Madame Lalaurie story, were also legendary, but Jeffries made her selections based on personal experience. We visited several stops on the tour where there had been reports of odd sounds and moving objects, leading Jeffries (who described herself as a little psychic) and her friend (described as very psychic) to investigate. Psychics can see and hear spirits that cause that kind of commotion, Jeffries explained. Sometimes spirits even pass through the bodies of the most sensitive psychics. The information that psychics glean from their encounters with the dead can then be pieced together with other kinds of evidence to build an understanding of whether sites were haunted and why. Her investigations of haunted places were "half psychic, half science," Karen explained. The teams she has worked with incorporated scientific methods by doing historical research and corroborating their conclusions with the findings of other paranormal investigators.

Our first stop on the tour was the Bourbon Orleans Hotel ballroom, which, Jeffries informed us, had been used for quadroon balls and Mardi Gras balls and to house an order of African American nuns. The space was "very haunted," she said, and to demonstrate the assertion, she would have us do an investigation. She brought out her ghost hunting tools and asked who wanted to use the thermodynamic detector. She taught us how to download the Ghost Radar app on our cell phones. I asked her why we needed all of this equipment in order to sense a ghost, and she replied that the tools are "more sensitive than we are." She explained that technology picks up images outside the light spectrum that we can't see, sounds from wavelengths that we can't hear, and energy fluctuations that we can't feel. Ghosts need energy in order to manifest, she told me. A cold spot is a ghost sucking energy out of that space. The more energy a ghost has, the more plainly it can manifest. It takes massive energy to project a total image, which is why people rarely see a full-on ghost.

While I chatted with Jeffries, my fellow tourists were fanning out around the room, monitoring the readings on their radars. Several folks were reporting blue spots (which indicate low energy), red spots (which indicate high energy), and unspoken spirit words flashing across their gadget screens that were somehow being picked up by the detectors. The center of the ballroom seemed to produce the highest number of energy spikes. Jeffries soon revealed the reason: black female ghosts from the nineteenth century were causing the disturbance. Jeffries explained that African American women of partial white "blood"—"quadroons, octoroons, and mulats"—used to attend quadroon balls to meet their "protectors," wealthy white men who would take them as mistresses. These men might find true love with their mistresses and maintain two families, Jeffries said. She knew from her paranormal investigations that "two quadroons" haunt the ballroom today: one was a matchmaker of mistresses and their "protectors," and one was returning to the spot where she had "met her true love and been happiest."

After learning about the lovelorn black women ghosts, we packed our equipment and headed downstairs to the hotel lobby, where Jeffries asked if any of us had ever experienced a haunting. Several people told sincere, personal stories of fearful occurrences or loved ones returned. More seemed eager to share, but it was time for us to leave the haunted hotel and head to our next stop. As we walked the streets of the French Quarter, lit up with bright lights, music, and revelry, Jeffries offered tidbits on the culture and history of early New Orleans. At one point she directed us to stop and sit on the broad courthouse steps, where she gave a rousing, lightning-quick history of the city, emphasizing the fire of 1788 as the root cause of many contemporary hauntings. Her spirited lecture was the highlight of the evening, inspiring the group to burst into spontaneous applause. She later paused by a Voodoo shop to talk about slavery, which had not come up in the history lecture. She mentioned the travesty of the Middle Passage (but not of slavery on Louisiana soil) and said that African beliefs had merged into Voodoo in the Americas, creating "a positive religion, a religion of light that was open to anyone." To illustrate this point, she described a Voodoo priestess she knew who was "a short Jewish woman from Maine." Jeffries cautioned us against "hoodoo," which she described as pertaining to hex spells and gris-gris bags, and said real Voodoo items need to be made by a priestess. When someone asked where one could get these "real" items, Jeffries recommended Rev. Zombie's Voodoo shop, right where we happened to be standing, or Marie Laveau's House of Voodoo, owned by the same person.

The final and most dramatic stop on Jeffries's tour pertained to the story of the infamous Creole slaveholder Madame Lalaurie. She halted our group in front of the Cabildo, the former seat of Spanish colonial government in New Orleans and location of the prison in the city's early Anglo-American period, to tell us about the mutilated slaves of Madame Lalaurie who were rescued and then housed there. Jeffries began by explaining that the Lalaurie story has turned into an urban legend, making it hard to separate lore from truth. Delphine Lalaurie, she told us, was a wealthy woman known by neighbors to be abusive to her slaves. A young slave girl had lost her life as a result of Lalaurie's cruelty. After inadvertently tugging a tangle while combing her mistress's hair, the girl ran wildly through the house trying to escape the punishing whip wielded by her mistress. A relentless Lalaurie chased the child to the roof, where the girl fell to her death. Jeffries said that a few years after that incident, a black woman cook who was chained to the stove started a fire in the Lalaurie house. Firefighters responding to the emergency found seven slaves dehydrated and starving in the upper-level slave-quarter apartment. The slave woman confessed to setting the fire in order to expose Madame Lalaurie even though she knew it might mean her own death. The abused slaves were taken to the Cabildo, while an angry mob of 2,000 people gathered at Lalaurie's home. The mob was incensed because Lalaurie's actions had crossed the line of acceptability even though many other masters also abused their slaves. Lalaurie avoided vigilante justice, Jeffries told our group, and was whisked away by coach to Lake Ponchartrain before escaping to Paris.

Then Jeffries confided to us that the deceased Madame Lalaurie used to haunt her. The haunting had ensued after Jeffries had entered the Lalaurie home with another psychic and author Carolyn Long several years prior. Jeffries described going upstairs in the house and immediately feeling the spirit of Delphine Lalaurie "pushing her backwards." Jeffries asked Lalaurie if she "did it," if she tortured her slaves, to which Lalaurie's spirit responded: "Yes! I did what I wanted with my animals, my pets." Jeffries then went into the "slave room" and "felt presences" there. She asked the slave spirits why they were confined, and a woman said it was because they had fallen "out of favor with Madame." Concerned for the trapped spirits, Jeffries began a ceremony to "send them home," but Lalaurie's ghost appeared at the door to prohibit her. Afterward, the spiteful Delphine Lalaurie followed Jeffries home, appearing in the mirrors of her house. Jeffries fell ill due to the personal haunting; her finances collapsed. Desperate, she asked a "priestess" to detach her from Delphine and then visited a Catholic priest, who conducted a cleansing that finally freed her from the evil spirit's hold.

After the tour, a handful of people stayed behind to tell their personal haunting stories, to ask Jeffries where they could get reliable psychic readings, and to inquire about authentic Voodoo items. Karen Jeffries had described her own beliefs and experiences, no matter how unusual, in a manner that seemed genuine. I felt that she was being sincere during the tour, that she believed in these spirit entities and their power. Before I began my solo walk back to the Hotel Monteleone, I asked Jeffries how she protects herself from ghosts. She said, "I pray for Jesus to bring light around me" and that she has someone with strong powers wave her with a salt wand. Like Karen Jeffries, many Americans believe in the existence of things unseen: ghosts, angels, and demons. Anthropologist Tanya Luhrmann notes that three out of four Americans believe in the paranormal according to Gallup polling.[3] It is not so remarkable, given this ratio, that many of the tourists and tour guides that I met during my travels said they believed in ghosts. More striking to me was the fact that two very different New Orleans paranormal tours kept returning to the subject of black history. The mainstream Gray Line cemetery tour was dominated by the mystique of Voodoo rituals and Marie Laveau. Karen Jeffries's independent tour began and ended with stories of blacks in the nineteenth century. Her rosy rendition of quadroon balls, while romanticizing the limited and often coerced sexual options of women of color in a patriarchal white supremacist social system, had made those women the objects of a hands-on ghost investigation.[4] Her concluding, rather shocking story about Delphine Lalaurie had centered on abused slaves and her own torment at the hands of a maniacal ghost mistress. Both of these tours dealt extensively with the role of race and slavery in the New Orleans past, and both incorporated sites and objects related to the famous story of slaveholder Madame Delphine Lalaurie. Madame Lalaurie, it became clear to me as I experienced haunted New Orleans, was the city's gruesome paranormal poster child, and it was she whom I would have to track down next.

The Famous "Haunted House" of Madame Lalaurie

Madame Delphine Macarty Lalaurie was a wealthy slaveholder and society maven of antebellum New Orleans. She was born into the Creole class of families descended from French or Spanish colonists who had arrived in the middle 1700s.[5] Charged with chaining, torturing, and deforming slaves in the attic of her fashionable Vieux Carré (French Quarter) townhouse, Lalaurie has been described over time as having a host of ironical traits. According to Louisiana lore, in the 1700s the Queen of Spain deemed Lalaurie "so beautiful" that she granted the wish of a pardon for Lalaurie's first husband, who had married the young belle without the required permission of the Crown.[6] In his classic 1888 book, *Strange True Tales of Louisiana*, George Washington Cable portrayed Lalaurie as a "fair," possibly "insane" lady of the "Creole pure-blood," with "pretty manners and sweetness of mien." Barbara Sillery, author of the PBS documentary and companion book *The Haunting of Louisiana* (2001), called Lalaurie "sadistic," "insidious," and "maniacal."[7] Commentators past and present agree that Madame Delphine Macarty Lalaurie was lovely, crazy, and also deadly.

On a sultry evening during that autumn trip, I heard a full and most fanciful telling of the Madame Lalaurie story. The French Quarter shone like an antique jewel box that night, its strands of shops and eateries aglow like so many sparkling beads. The sidewalks overflowed with humanity: locals, tourists, and street performers. Those of us who had bought tickets online for the Haunted History Tour cued up outside Rev. Zombie's Voodoo shop on St. Peter Street. Others joined us to buy their tickets from an attendant dressed all in black. We were then directed to wait across the road, in front of Pat O'Brien's Bar, home of the famous Hurricane drink. As the size of our group grew, those of us already present affixed Haunted History stickers to our shirts and waved paper fans shaped like skulls. "You don't see that in Ohio!" a member of the group called out, pointing to a figure on stilts whose bizarre, brightly colored full-body costume made him or her appear like a demon from outer space. Just as the oddly discomfiting figure disappeared into the Voodoo shop, our tour group set off, moving past a colorful array of visually arresting structures. Due to a series of fires that destroyed the city's original French buildings in the late 1700s, the architecture of the French Quarter is principally Spanish Colonial, replete with charming galleries and porches, fanciful detailing, and elaborate ironwork.

Haunted History Tour sign, New Orleans. Customers waiting to take the Haunted History Tour in New Orleans meet by this sign in front of a Voodoo shop in the French Quarter. Photo by the author, 2013.

Our tour guide (we'll call him Jean, with a French pronunciation), told us up front that he was a New Orleans native of French ancestry. He wore his sable hair in long, romantic waves and was dressed in a white shirt with puffed sleeves paired with a black vest and trousers. Similar in looks to the romance-novel cover model Fabio, Jean was dramatic in his storytelling style, insistent at times, yet controlled when the story required it, all the while turning on and off a robust French accent for ambience and flair. He began the tour with safety tips, telling the group to stay out of the street, sound advice for many members of our party who were gaily sipping on Hurricanes. "People think New Orleans is Disneyland for adults," Jean told us, "but it's not. These horse-drawn carriages will run you over." He then invited us to use any technology we had brought along and explained how EMF meters work to signal the electromagnetic presence of ghosts. He proclaimed New Orleans "the most haunted city in America" and challenged Savannah's title to the name. "Savannah likes to claim it is the most haunted city of America," he said, "but they don't have the history. In Savannah, they lie."

Jean suavely guided us through the shadowed French Quarter streets, counting down the top reasons why New Orleans is so haunted. He said the settlement was built on the sacred ground of "cannibal Indians," and so the land was cursed. It was also, and not coincidentally, the location of two great fires, in 1788 and 1794, which broke out exactly where the cannibal rituals had been performed. The high death toll of one of those fires could have been averted, Jean said, if only the priest had not padded the bells and prevented their use as a warning for those in the pathway of the flames. As Jean told stories of ghostly schoolchildren, nuns, and pirates, he said New Orleans had been a medieval city once, with torturous punishments and public hangings meted out on the now bucolic Jackson Square. He also explained his interesting theory that "residual hauntings" are actually replays of history, caused by the dead person's emotions being imprinted and fixed in natural building materials (like limestone) and later released by humidity.

The tale of Delphine Lalaurie's house was the culmination of Jean's Haunted History tour. He began by warning our group that this story was far worse than any we had heard thus far. Madame Delphine Lalaurie was like a princess in New Orleans, he said, hailing from one of the wealthiest families of the Creole elite. She was a willful, spiteful, dark-haired beauty with an arrogant personality. She was filthy rich and owned at least $5 million, which amounted to about half of the U.S.

Treasury at the time. She was a hostess of lavish society parties, and no one dared to offend her for fear of never being invited back.

During one of these parties, a slave boy rushed into the parlor, trying to get Madame's attention. She ignored him at first, causing him to touch her, an affront to her delicate sensibilities. Insistent, the boy informed his mistress that the kitchen was on fire. Her reaction was simply to move the party outside onto Royal Street and command the musicians to keep playing. Firemen soon arrived on the scene only to discover a seventy-year-old Haitian cook chained to a cast-iron stove inside the house. Since the chain and stove both conducted heat, the woman's flesh had been cooking a little bit each day. As the firemen searched the house for more slaves, a horrible stench of human blood, urine, and feces wafted from the third-floor slave quarters, causing the firemen to vomit. They forced the door open and found four slaves inside. One had his skin peeled and tongue cut out and was covered in maggots such that his entire face looked white; one had her joints cracked and was crawling like an inch worm; one woman was folded into herself and stuffed into a box; finally, chained to an operating table was a barely recognizable man with missing eyes and ears and no nose who had been experimented on for a crude sex change. All of the mutilated slaves were brought down to the street and laid on straw in front of the partygoers.

Local residents took offense at the sight of these atrocities, especially as this kind of treatment was illegal in the city. New Orleans was different from the rest of the South, our tour guide explained. Here slaves had protection and a chance to acquire their freedom, such that they would not want to run. It seemed to New Orleans residents like hell had opened up inside the Lalaurie mansion in order for abuses like these to occur there, Jean said. Nevertheless, the party guests hesitated to make the offenses public because of Madame's power. An editor of the New Orleans newspaper who was a guest at the party finally came forward to tell the story. Madame Lalaurie emerged from the house then, curtsied to the gathering crowd of angry residents, and was whisked away to safety by her black slave coachman, Bastille. An angry mob attacked the house, ripping the tainted structure apart and destroying the fine, imported furnishings.

No one thought to search the premises, our tour guide continued, so they did not know that Madame Lalaurie had buried twelve slaves alive beneath the floorboards just before she left her mansion that day. After the fire, onlookers heard muted voices in French and Spanish coming from the house. Then they heard guttural, demonic sounds. The buried-alive slaves, who had been smuggled into the country illegally, were finally at death's door and speaking in their natal West African tongue, the language of Voodoo. Years later, human bones marred by tooth marks were discovered on the property, evidence that in their final hours, the slaves had resorted to cannibalism.

Over the years there have been numerous hauntings at the Lalaurie house, our guide intoned, winding down his gruesome tale. A white male resident once saw a black man's ghost near the former slave quarters. The ghost held his mouth open in a silent scream, revealing a nub in the back of his mouth where his tongue should have been. Another white man who ran a furniture store out of the lower level of the home twice had his wares mysteriously soiled with feces, blood, and urine. The actor Nicolas Cage used to own the house, but he refused to ever sleep in it. Why? The answer would be left to our imaginations. Jean ended his tour with a reminder that Savannah has nothing on New Orleans when it comes to hauntings and advised our group to tip the tour guide in order to prevent child ghosts from following us home.

Although Jean's version was certainly the most artful, I heard the story of Madame Lalaurie's haunted house told several times and in various ways during my travels to New Orleans, often without even trying to. Once I ventured to the Lalaurie mansion, a private residence now, to take photographs on a late Sunday afternoon. I happened upon a crowd gathered at the Royal and Governor Nicholls Streets intersection where the foreboding gray townhouse stands. Most of the people on the corner were balancing awkwardly on black motorized scooters. A tour guide similarly equipped (and who I could not help but think might have been the son of my previous Save Our Cemeteries guide) had the crowd enthralled. Passersby paused to catch a bit of the tour guide's narrative. "We should listen in on this tour," I heard a young woman whisper to her traveling companions. "They're talking about La-lau-rie." She spoke the name in a hushed tone and exaggerated French accent meant to connote intrigue. The tour guide was just getting to the part about the tortured slaves on whom Madame Lalaurie had performed twisted medical experiments. The crowd stood with rapt attention, listening to detailed coverage of the mutilations visited upon helpless bondspeople and proving that Lalaurie's story was just as captivating in 2013 as it had been more than 100 years before, when reports of her evil deeds spread like the flames that claimed her massive house.

British travel writer and antislavery advocate Harriet Martineau was the first to pen a cohesive narrative about the Lalaurie scandal.[8] During her visit to New Orleans in 1838, Martineau observed the "ruined" house on Royal Street and inquired about its history. She gathered information from local residents and published what she learned in the final chapter of her *Retrospect of Western Travel* (1838–40). As she recounted for readers the experience of driving down "the road to the lake on a fine afternoon," Martineau reflected on Madame Lalaurie's escape down that very road five years prior. "The remembrance or tradition of that day will always be fresh in New-Orleans," Martineau wrote; "it is a revelation of what may happen in a slaveholding country, and can happen nowhere else."[9] Martineau described Lalaurie as a "French creole" who was "so graceful and accomplished, so charming in her manners and so hospitable, that no one ventured openly to question her perfect goodness." Nevertheless, Martineau contended, Lalaurie was primarily responsible for keeping her slaves in a "haggard and wretched condition," with the exception of Lalaurie's coachman, who was "sleek and comfortable enough." According to Martineau, Lalaurie also abused her daughters and enjoyed torturing her slaves. Martineau included the story of the cook chained to the stove who purposely set the house on fire, of wild and starving slaves in chains discovered in the home, of the mob's fury and destruction of the house, and finally, of Lalaurie's swift escape. It was Martineau who first wrote down the incident about the small slave girl who lost her life after being chased to the rooftop by Lalaurie, a detail that is not corroborated by other primary sources. A neighbor, Martineau claimed, had been witness to the entire event, from the frenzied chase inside the house to the illicit burial of the child in the courtyard that evening.[10] This eight-year-old slave child would be the first ghost that another witness, a young white girl, reported seeing at the house fifty years later, as told by journalist George Washington Cable.

In the 1880s, George Washington Cable retold the Lalaurie tale in his popular collection of "true" Louisiana stories, raising the profile of the house and its nefarious mistress at the turn of a new century. In his riveting rendition, which incurred the ire of some New Orleans elites for its criticism of Delphine Lalaurie, Cable turned the home into a character equal in intrigue to its owner. After pages of description of the home's balconies, walls, windows, ceilings, and eerie doors that unlatched themselves, Cable approached the heart of the home's darkness: the slave quarters in the belvedere. He wrote, "Wings of that sort were once very common in New Orleans in the residences of the rich; they were the house's slave quarters. But certainly some of the features you see here never were common—locks seven inches across; several windows without sashes, but with sturdy iron gratings and solid iron shutters."[11] Cable went on to describe the "full length batten shutters" attached by "iron hooks" that closed off the doorway of the slave quarters. It was through this doorway, he noted, that "the ghosts . . . got into the house." This moment is one of four when Cable mentions ghosts in the mansion, and with each comment he equivocates, noting that these are figurative ghosts, as his tale only deals with "plain fact and history."[12] With this skillful touch of ambivalence, Cable is able to preserve his reputation as a journalist and his claim that the tales are based on fact while also affirming, and indeed spreading, public belief in the haunted house.

Only after describing the prisonlike house does Cable narrate the cruel misdeeds of Delphine Lalaurie. Much of what he says we have already encountered in Martineau's narrative, as well as in the contemporary ghost tours previously described that build on the work of these early writers. It is important to this discussion, though, to highlight the details of Cable's popular and influential version. Cable acknowledged racial and sexual tension in New Orleans society by describing Madame Lalaurie as a member of the Creole female elite who "hated" the "quadroon caste" of mixed-race women, competitors for the erotic attention of white men. He also repeated Martineau's observation about the animosity between Creole Catholic elites and Protestant Anglo-American elites who had flooded the city in the years following the Louisiana Purchase of 1803. Again, borrowing from Martineau, he asserted that Lalaurie controlled her husband, the French-born medical doctor Louis Lalaurie, who was "younger" and "of lesser importance."[13] Cable wrote that during the fire, as Madame Lalaurie deflected the rescuers' questions about slaves in the house and directed them instead to save her expensive furnishings, her husband only stood by, "passive as ever."[14] In contrast to the feckless Louis Lalaurie, Cable positioned the black slave coachman, unnamed in his version, as a male figure on whom Delphine Lalaurie doted and depended. In short, Cable captured a social scene brewing with latent conflict about race, gender, class, and ethno-national issues.

At the conclusion of his tale, Cable traced the evolution of the Lalaurie house into an experimental interracial high school for girls (quickly shut down in the 1870s) and finally described the home's stint as a conservatory for music. Through it all, Cable hinted at the presence of ghosts in the building: a female specter glimpsed on the roof by a neighbor girl, a fear of ghosts harbored by the high school boarding students, and the "ghosts walking on the waves of harmony" during conservatory musical performances. "The place," he wrote, "came to be looked on as haunted."[15]

George Washington Cable drew liberally on Harriet Martineau's work, adding fleeting mentions of ghosts as only a local could and turning the Lalaurie story into a legendary portrait of early New Orleans.[16] Successive writers and folklorists elaborated on Cable's tale, layering in wilder and more extreme elements. In 1945 the Louisiana Writers' Project folklore collection highlighted "The famous 'Haunted House' of Madame Lalaurie" in a section called "Ghosts." The house was "undoubtedly the best known of those in this oldest section of the city, [and] has been so much publicized that there is no use repeating here its controversial tale of slave-torture, flight and envy," the writers stated. Despite the claim of the WPA writers that the tale need not be repeated, their collection recounts the Lalaurie story in a separate section titled "The Slaves."[17] Perhaps inspired by the WPA folklore collection, fiction writer Jeanne deLavigne published *Ghost Stories of Old New Orleans* (1946), in which she inserted the gruesome details about medical experiments on slaves retained in many of the present-day Lalaurie house ghost-tour narratives. In the story "The Haunted House of the Rue Royale," deLavigne painted a lavish picture of Lalaurie and her luxurious home, which stood in stark contrast to the suffering slaves within, who were "stark naked, chained to the wall, their eyes gouged out, their fingernails pulled off by the roots . . . their ears hanging by shreds, their lips sewed together, their tongues drawn out and sewed to their chins, severed hands stitched to bellies, legs pulled joint from joint." Her narrative, which continued in horribly imaginative detail, was accompanied by graphic drawings of tortured and mutilated slave bodies. DeLavigne also embellished the ghost stories that Cable had treated only gingerly. She described the "grisly" ghost of the slave girl who came "shrieking through the shrill air" from the rooftop of the mansion on moonlit nights and the "black ghosts and white ghosts" who "besieged" the poor Italian immigrants who rented rooms in the house in the late 1800s.[18] Historical novels were later written about Lalaurie (Barbara Hambly's *Fever Season* and T. R. Heinan's *L'Immortalite: Madame Lalaurie and the Voodoo Queen*), as was a graphic novel

(Serena Valentino's *Nightmares and Fairytales: 1140 Rue Royale*) in which the slave ghosts rise to take revenge on Madame Lalaurie upon her return from Paris.[19] A Google search will turn up gory drawings from deLavigne's book, still-life images from the Museé Conti Historical Wax Museum in New Orleans (which shows Lalaurie's wax figure dressed in a pink gown and bending toward her tortured slaves), contemporary amateur artists' renderings of Madame Lalaurie (one of which transforms her into a dark, knife-wielding, anime-like occult heroine), and myriad "ghost photos" of Lalaurie's haunted house.

Barbarous and Fiendish Atrocities

Two recent works of history seriously investigate the Lalaurie case. *Mad Madame Lalaurie* (2011), by historian Victoria Cosner Love and novelist Lorelei Shannon, outlines factual and fictional versions of the story. The authors track various claims that have been woven into Lalaurie lore over the years, including Dr. Louis Lalaurie's use of "zombie drugs" to make slaves more compliant, the assistance that he is said to have received from "voodoo queen" Marie Laveau, and Madame Lalaurie's adoption of the "Devil Baby" monster-child brought to her by Laveau to care for. Love and Shannon conclude that these claims are not supported by evidence. The authors argue that Lalaurie was aware of the condition of her slaves and was involved in their mistreatment to some degree, but they dispute that "she was the legendary monster she has been made out to be."[20]

A second book, Carolyn Morrow Long's *Madame Lalaurie: Mistress of the Haunted House* (2012), is the most thoroughly researched and extensive treatment of Lalaurie's history to date. It is from Long's careful archival research, as well as original newspaper reportage of the 1834 incident, that we can draw a clearer picture of the events that inspired subsequent ghost stories. As Long recounts, Madame Lalaurie was born Marie Delphine Macarty in the late 1700s to a wealthy New Orleans family of French and Irish ancestry. Prior to Delphine's birth, New Orleans came under Spanish rule when the French handed over the colony of Louisiana to Spain in 1763. Delphine therefore came of age under a Spanish political regime in a social world with deep French roots. She lived with her family on a large plantation of 1,344 acres worked by twenty-four slaves of African descent. The Macarty plantation, located on the outskirts of New Orleans, produced indigo, sugar, and cotton.

The teenaged Delphine married López y Ángulo, a Spanish officer and second in command to the Louisiana governor. He died five years later in a shipwreck before Delphine gave birth to their first child in Cuba.[21]

Delphine returned to New Orleans in 1805, two years after the United States had purchased the colony of Louisiana from France (which had secretly gotten it back from Spain). American planters and government officials swept into the rich agricultural region of the Mississippi Delta, raising tensions between Anglo newcomers and French and Spanish elites. As a very young woman, Delphine married again, to the French-born merchant and black-market slave smuggler Jean Paul Blanque. After her mother's death, Delphine received a sizable inheritance including a plantation on the Mississippi River, fifty-two slaves, livestock, and farm equipment. Her father then gave the newlyweds another plantation and furnishings, a lot in town, and twenty-six slaves, making Delphine a millionaire by today's monetary standards. When her husband died at age fifty, Delphine was widowed again with five children. Carolyn Long lists by name the twenty enslaved women, men, and children left in Delphine's possession after her husband's passing. (Notably, a man named Bastien is listed as her twenty-two-year-old carpenter, coach driver, and domestic). In 1819 Delphine freed a slave, Jean Louis, in accordance with her late husband's wishes. However, eight other slaves had died in her household (likely of disease and complications of childbirth), and she would soon be accused of slave abuse.[22]

In 1828 Delphine married a third time, to French doctor Louis Lalaurie, a twenty-five-year-old younger man. Five months prior to the nuptials, she had given birth to their son. The couple's age difference was so great and, indeed, unusual in its gender arrangement that Louis Lalaurie's father back in France had originally thought Delphine was acting as a surrogate maternal figure for his son. The couple at first resided on Delphine's Mississippi River plantation in what was, according to a nearby French businessman, a relationship characterized by discord and frequent separations. In the first year of her marriage, Delphine was investigated for cruelty toward her slaves and then immediately sold six enslaved people to her friend, perhaps to avoid further trouble in the matter. Although no court records exist for this slave abuse case, Carolyn Long uncovered a document showing Lalaurie's payment of legal fees for her defense in an unspecified criminal case in 1829. In all likelihood, Delphine did defend herself against criminal charges of slave abuse and sold a group of slaves as a result of that case.[23]

In 1831, the Lalauries moved into the now legendary house at 1140 Royal Street. In contrast to the tall and austere gray home that tourists see today, which features extensive renovations conducted after the fire, the original home had two stories, an attic, and a hipped roof with dormers, balconies, and wrought-iron railings. According to Long, the Lalauries "lived lavishly in their new home" and "held extravagant parties to which the best society of New Orleans were invited." Despite this aura of gaiety, Delphine petitioned the court for a separation from her husband in 1832, charging that he "beat and wound her in the most outrageous and cruel manner" and that there were witnesses to his actions. The couple separated, reconciled, and was again cohabitating on Royal Street at the time of the conflagration.[24]

Two New Orleans newspapers, the *Louisiana Courier* and the *New Orleans Bee*, reported that on the morning of April 10, 1834, the Lalaurie kitchen burst into flames. The kitchen was located in the service wing of the house, below the slave quarters, which would have put the bondspeople at greatest risk. The fire drew a large crowd to the residence, leading to the discovery of "barbarous and fiendish atrocities committed by the woman Lalaurie upon the persons of her slaves," as described in the *Bee*. On April 11 the paper printed that "several gentlemen impelled by their feelings of humanity" pressed into the house despite the Lalauries' overt lack of concern for their slaves and found "inmates of the premises . . . incarcerated therein." The newspaper reported that "seven slaves, more or less horribly mutilated, were seen suspended by the neck, with their limbs apparently stretched and torn from one extremity to the other." A criminal court judge who had joined the crowd outside the burning house gave a deposition that was printed in the newspaper. Judge Jacques Francois Canonge stated that the Lalauries denied there were slaves inside who were at risk from the fire and charged they were being slandered. Upon hearing that slaves had been discovered in the home, the judge reported giving an order to have the locked doors forced open. He described the discovery of three enslaved women, one with "an iron collar very large and heavy . . . chained with heavy irons by the feet. That she walked with the greatest difficulty." Another woman was quite old with "a deep wound on the head." The injured slaves were removed to the mayor's office in the Cabildo, where, the *Bee* reported, 4,000 residents of the city later came to view them. The crowd outside the Lalaurie home quickly turned violent, unleashing "a popular fury" that was described as "the first act of its kind that our populace ever engaged in." Outraged by the slaves' mistreatment, the mob ransacked what remained of the elegant townhouse, dashing valuable furnishings to the ground and defiling the walls with graffiti.[25]

After the incident, Delphine Lalaurie removed to Paris. Love and Shannon posit that she later returned to New Orleans. Long writes that Lalaurie was buried in Paris in 1849 but that her remains were later exhumed. Long concludes that in 1851, Lalaurie's bones were placed in a tomb etched with the words "tombe de familie" and owned by Paulin Blanque. The tomb is located in New Orleans Cemetery No. 1.[26]

According to many believers today, Madame Delphine Lalaurie's ghost still haunts her city of old and tortures the spirits of former slaves. In the book *The Haunting of Louisiana*, Sillery concludes her chapter on the Lalaurie mansion with a foreboding note: "There have been reports of recent sightings of the sadistic ghost of Madame Lalaurie returning to her former home. Masking her identity behind a dark veil of Spanish lace, she slithers by, eavesdropping at shuttered windows for the tormented cries of her mutilated slaves."[27] And Karen Jeffries shared at the end of her tour that she has had personal encounters with Lalaurie's ghost. Long concludes her biography of Delphine Lalaurie by describing what appears to be the same event that led to Jeffries's haunting trials. Long writes that in 2009 she visited the Lalaurie home with "some friends who are professional psychics." The friends, Karen Jeffries, Juliet Pazera, and Mary Millan (who runs haunted tours under the professional name Bloody Mary and is described as a "priestess of Voudou"), all had paranormal experiences in the home. Pazera saw the spirit of Lalaurie, which "pervades the whole block." Millan "came into contact with the spirits of several enslaved persons." Jeffries saw the upper space "filled with slaves, wailing, their hands in the air reaching up to heaven." In her vision, the slaves were "crying and praying for help. The pain is terrible. They will never live through this." When Jeffries asked the slave spirits if they wished to speak, a man named Marquette came forward and described Lalaurie. "The mistress is polish and beauty on the outside," he said, "but on the inside, she is like the sleek panther. . . . She enjoys the kill and watches the twisting and writhing of the victim." Marquette refused to leave the house, Jeffries learned, because he vowed to see his former mistress pay for her cruelty. Finally, Jeffries communicated with the spirit of a "kitchen slave" who said, "I just keeps my mouth shut. . . . Madame has slapped me, but I cook good so she don't hurt me much." Psychic Juliet Pazera sensed still more slaves at the front of the house during this visit—spirits heavy with "despair" and "crouched down with fear." Long ends her book by stating that while none of these spirit entities can be positively identified, they hold certain resemblances to Lalaurie's documented slaves.[28]

Jeffries's and Long's separate reports of communication with slave ghosts at the Lalaurie mansion display empathy for the enslaved and a desire to elicit their stories. The encounters they describe therefore reflect an improvement on the representation of Lalaurie's slave ghosts in Sillery's book (where the slaves are still threatened by their mistress) and on the Haunted History Tour (where one enslaved ghost is literally mute, with his tongue removed). However, even the empathetic portrayals of slave specters in Long's epilogue reproduce troubling dynamics. Although the psychics ask the slaves to speak, thereby offering them the agency that comes with voice, speech is only possible through mediums: psychics not of African descent, at least two of whom lead ghost tours in the city. Black slaves' stories of suffering, accommodation, and even defiance are thus filtered through professionals with a commercial interest in the ghost-tourism trade. And as the Lalaurie case clearly shows, this commercial interest centers on graphic portrayals of violence against people of African descent who can never really defend themselves, either as slaves during the antebellum era or as ghosts today.

Mad Woman in the Attic

Replete with horror, broken taboos, grotesque bodies, and racialized subjection, the Lalaurie mansion on Royal Street is a dark-tourism magnet. Consumers of the Lalaurie tours and tale can engage in an experience that allows for a dalliance with—and disassociation from— troubling historical realities. The Lalaurie story turns on crimes of racial violence, a kind of violence that our post–civil rights society rightly and vociferously rejects. In other, more mainstream social circumstances, listeners might feel self-conscious or even ashamed for enjoying the recounting of such brutal acts. However, the popularized Lalaurie tale includes within it an easy means for the dissolution of critical self-awareness. By participating in the castigation of a vicious slave mistress with whom they have nothing in common, tourists can distance themselves from her actions and relieve themselves of personal responsibility for indulging in scenes of abuse, racism, and torture.

A preponderance of evidence from the 1830s does indicate that Delphine Lalaurie committed or at the very least permitted extreme physical abuse of the human beings she owned. At the same time, her infamy for these crimes makes her a ready scapegoat for those who enjoy, but also denounce, the horror of her behavior. To strike this delicate balance between fascination and castigation, purveyors of the Lalaurie story must create a means for listeners to distance themselves from Lalaurie's actions. Madame Lalaurie is therefore presented as an insane, sadistic sociopath who stood outside the norms of proper New Orleans society. And there is a subtle side benefit to this widespread positioning of Delphine Lalaurie as marginal and exceptional. Her unusual crimes can be divorced from mainstream New Orleans history, allowing New Orleans to maintain the reputation, often repeated by tour guides, as a good place to have been a slave. In order to protect listeners' pleasure in the gruesome tale of the house on Royal Street, as well as to preserve New Orleans's identity as an exceptional city where slavery was lenient, Madame Lalaurie's villainy must be idiosyncratic. Her actions, in other words, must clearly violate social norms both in her time and in our own.

The popular story told about Madame Delphine Lalaurie does this cultural work, establishing her as a mad and scheming misfit, the ultimate social "other." First, she is categorized as foreign in an Anglo-American context, a characteristic signaled by constant references to her French Creole identity. The notion that Lalaurie is not *really* American plays on latent ethnocentrism to partly explain her aberrant behavior. Second, she is described as a woman who does not meet idealized societal standards for her gender. While appearing to be the perfect picture of a graceful mistress of the manse, Lalaurie is actually an atrocious beast who uses her beauty to mask corruption. She somehow attracts and marries a much younger man and lords over him. Dr. Louis Lalaurie is rendered passive, even childlike, in the story. It is no wonder that he merely stands aside and watches as his strong-willed wife perpetrates atrocious acts, including the abuse of her own daughters. This unsexed French woman behaves like a man, dominating relationships and directing affairs in her household. Third, Delphine Lalaurie is deviant in her closeness to particular African Americans even as she tortures others. She is said to be especially solicitous of her enslaved coachman, whose "blackness" and "sleekness," and the implied sexuality relayed by those descriptors, are emphasized in George Washington Cable's account.[29] Cable's late-nineteenth-century narrative infused the relationship between Lalaurie and her coachman with a tinge of illicit desire across the color line, an unspoken suggestion that lingers in later versions. Because several cases of illegal "amalgamation" involving white women and black men were reported in New Orleans newspapers in the 1850s, Cable's insinuation carried an air of real possibility. In one particular case covered by the *Picayune*, police accused an elite white woman of intimate involvement with her black coachman.[30] Finally, Lalaurie is linked to Voodoo through her purported association with Marie Laveau and alleged adoption of the devil baby. It is perhaps not a stretch to argue that Lalaurie's unwomanly behavior, erotic connection with a black man, and adoption of a racialized monster child liken her to the stereotypical image of the black Mammy-matriarch who runs her family with an iron first, denying the black man his right to patriarchal privilege. Due to her Frenchness, gender nonconformity, and strange relations with African Americans that were at the same time too close and too cruel, Madame Delphine Lalaurie is portrayed as a person beyond the pale.

Delphine Lalaurie emerges, through the intersection of these deviant qualities, as an antiheroine of the slaveholding class. She is a wicked witch of the Western frontier, the evil villainess of grim fairy tales projected onto the history of American slavery. An elite French woman whose violent streak is said to be directly related to her ethnicity, Delphine Lalaurie can be figured as distinctive from traditional southern belles. Even biographer Long's well-researched book can be read as reinforcing a gendered ethnic stereotype, as she repeats the notion that Creole mistresses were especially cruel, citing three primary source examples. Long quotes a narrative about Louisiana plantations by French traveler Claude-Cézar Robin in which he describes Creole mistresses relishing the punishment of slaves. She cites the journal of American military officer Major Amos Stoddard, who reported that Creole women in Louisiana were "habitually cruel to their slaves." She also quotes American architect Benjamin Latrobe, who wrote that Creole women "can look on the tortures of their slaves, inflicted by their orders, with satisfaction, & coolly prescribe the dose of infliction."[31] While Long's examples cannot be disregarded, it is notable that all three of these sources date to the early period of American control in Louisiana, when tensions were high between French and Spanish elites and new American settlers. It is possible that the American observers were filtering impressions of Creole women through negative stereotypes of "foreign" femininity, which they in turn repeated in their narratives. The French commentator might be read, in contrast, as implicitly comparing Creole women in Louisiana not to American women but, instead, to French women in the home nation, where plantation slavery was not practiced. His comment, then, would not necessarily support the notion that Creole women were crueler mistresses than other women in the slaveholding South.

Indeed, historian Thavolia Glymph has demonstrated through the use of slave narratives and slaveholding women's diaries and letters that white women across the South were harsh and violent toward their slaves.[32] After conducting a broad survey of primary sources, Glymph records a catalog of abuses perpetrated by white women against enslaved African American children and adults. She writes that mistresses routinely "slapped, hit, and even brutally whipped their slaves" and records numerous examples of extreme and creative punishments ranging from burns to abuse that caused blindness. White slave mistresses also readily wielded their social power to orchestrate whippings of black slaves by white male slaveholders, often their husbands, and also by overseers. Although the "iconic image of the southern lady became a fixture of post-Reconstruction white supremacist campaigns," historical evidence demonstrates the actual abuses of power carried out by white women in slaveholding households.[33] Indeed, numerous Anglo-Protestant women were just as heartless as the images presented of Creole women by nineteenth-century observers.

Delphine Lalaurie's chaining, starving, and beating of slaves would fit right into Glymph's inventory of white women's treatment of their human chattel. However, the representation of Delphine Lalaurie as especially cruel because she was Creole preserves a space in the American cultural imagination for the idealized southern lady: a genteel Anglo-Protestant slave mistress who was fragile, pious, virtuous, pleasing, and positioned in a subordinate role in relation to her husband. As a woman who meets none of these criteria of the southern lady, Madame Delphine Lalaurie is easy to hate. It is telling, in this regard, that the documentary evidence of her own experience of physical abuse at the hands of her last husband has not gained traction in ghost-tour narratives.

In popular tales of the haunted house on Royal Street, Delphine Lalaurie is an outlier not only in contrast to female slaveholders as a group but also in contrast to other New Orleans residents. Her cruel behavior is portrayed as exceptional in relation to the norm of New Orleans slaveholding society, and the city itself is represented as a place where slavery was lenient. For as the Haunted History tour guide pointed out (twice), New Orleans was a place where "the law" is presumed to have protected slaves such that they would "have no need to run away." In a city where slavery was not so bad, the guide suggested, Lalaurie's use of chains and corporal punishment was a reflection of her immoral character rather than of a genuine need to control the action of slaves who might wish to seek freedom.

The notion that the city of New Orleans was a good place to be a slave recurs in all versions of the Lalaurie story. But the positive "laws" to which the Haunted History tour guide referred, and that other tellers of the Lalaurie tale emphasize as the reason for a lenient system of slavery, were neither comprehensive nor uniformly enforced. Louisiana's Code Noir was a legal code for the regulation of slavery developed for the French Caribbean colonies in 1685 and revised for Louisiana in 1724. It is crucial to note that in its systemization of slaveholding practices, the Code Noir explicitly sanctioned the ownership of human beings. The Code Noir was rooted in the French objective to permit, shape, and control a form of slavery heavily influenced by Catholic religious principles. Catholicism, and hence the Code Noir, disallowed the separation of enslaved family members by sale and prohibited labor on Sundays. This latter provision in the code led to the practice of slaves gathering on Sundays in New Orleans's Congo Square to socialize, trade, and dance. These were, in fact, relatively permissive aspects of the code that created greater security for enslaved families and allowed for critical cultural exchange among blacks. The French Code Noir (as well as the Catholic-influenced Spanish legal code that operated for a generation in Louisiana in the late 1700s) also forbade "barbarous and inhumane" treatment of slaves. However, it did not forbid corporal punishment on the part of individual slaveholders or on the part of representatives of the colonial government.[34] In addition, the prohibition against torture and murder in the code often went unenforced, such that extreme beatings, mutilations, and even deaths were amply documented in New Orleans and surrounding plantations.[35] In addition to allowances for physical punishment in the Louisiana slave code, New Orleans was home to the largest slave market in the nation from the early 1800s until the Civil War, and hence it became a public stage for a debased objectification of African American men, women, and children.[36] While slavery in New Orleans was distinctive from slavery in other American colonies and early states due to the contingencies of colonial history, economic trends, and religious authority, it was still slavery. Indeed, one of the largest slave uprisings in American history took place on the outskirts of New Orleans in 1811. The assembled group of 400 to 500 slaves assaulted slaveholders, beat drums, waved banners, and were attempting to march into the city before they were halted and eventually punished by U.S. troops and local militia.

Tour guides and authors frame the destruction of Lalaurie's house as proof that antebellum New Orleanians could not abide slave abuse. While it is striking that a multitude of New Orleans residents gathered to express outrage at the treatment of slaves in 1834 just as the abolitionist movement was gathering strength in the North, one wishes the primary accounts described in detail the racial and class makeup of the protestors. The "popular fury" likely consisted of people from multiracial and multiethnic backgrounds, blacks, free people of color, Creoles, white Americans, and possibly Native Americans.[37] Certainly, though, these were not slaveholding elites, as newspaper coverage indicates that city authorities read the crowd "the riot act" in an attempt to exert control before the mob devolved into a widespread attack on slaveholders. A newspaper account just days after the event stated that the crowd planned "to wreak their vengeance on other persons accused of being guilty of similar conduct as that of Mde. Lalaurie."[38] British traveler Harriet Martineau also indicated that "the crowd at first intended to proceed to the examination of other premises, whose proprietors were under suspicion of cruelty to their slaves."[39] It is apparent in these accounts that contrary to how the Lalaurie story is told, Delphine Lalaurie was not viewed as exceptional by other New Orleans residents. Rather, she was understood to be part of an unnumbered group of slaveholders who practiced cruelty without penalty.

Madame Delphine Lalaurie is consistently described as "mad" and "insane" in published treatments of her history. In the garret of her urban mansion, she is said to have committed the vilest acts of sadistic lunacy. But instead of Madame Lalaurie being a rare type of slave mistress in a rare type of slave society, historical evidence suggests that she was among many in the New Orleans area and greater South who treated African Americans like chattel, and often brutally so. Entertaining stories of the haunted house on Royal Street depend on the vilification of their central character, Madame Lalaurie, whose guilt absolves New Orleans slaveholders in the past and the New Orleans tourist industry in the present from responsibility for committing or sensationalizing acts of racialized violence.

Madame Delphine Lalaurie was made legendary in the late 1800s by George Washington Cable's *Strange True Tales of Louisiana*, after which a local businessman attempted to capitalize on the notoriety of the haunted house by charging an entry fee.[40] In 2013–14, Lalaurie was catapulted back into the limelight due to the success of the FX television show *American Horror Story*. Set in New Orleans for its third season, *American Horror Story* followed a coven of witches descended from the Salem witches of lore. The combination of setting, story line, and a star-studded cast including Kathy Bates, Jessica Lange, and Angela Bassett produced a 75 percent increase in ratings for the series.[41]

The young witches on the show live in a secret boarding school run by a powerful witch and her selfish, youth-obsessed, even more powerful mother. The Salem witches of the boarding school (all white save one) are in conflict with the Voodoo witches of the beauty shop who live in the black section of town. Marie Laveau, head of the Voodoo witches, has magically extended her life since the 1800s and retained her youthful beauty by way of a secret that the senior Salem witch passionately covets. The first episode of the series sets the stage for the witches' entangled drama by flashing back in time to early New Orleans and the luxurious mansion of Madame Lalaurie. Startling scenes dramatize a house of horrors where Lalaurie verbally abuses her daughters and maliciously tortures her slaves. In the dim attic where slaves are kept half-clothed and chained, Lalaurie delights in their torment. Madame Lalaurie (played by Kathy Bates) forces her daughter to cut out the spleen of a slave, from which Lalaurie makes a poultice of blood and body tissue. Lalaurie smears the vile concoction on her face to keep her skin young before descending her grand staircase for a party. Later Lalaurie orders that a bull's head be placed on the slave (named Bastille after the black coachman of Lalaurie lore) whose spleen she took, turning him into a hybrid beast, a Minotaur. Bastille is said to be the lover of Marie Laveau, who retaliates against Lalaurie by killing her with a poisonous antiaging potion. At the end of this episode, time flashes forward to the present to show the young Salem boarding school witches touring Madame Lalaurie's historic home. One of the witches hears an unnatural sound—Lalaurie in her grave—whereupon the senior white witch raises Lalaurie from the dead and forces her back to the boarding school. Wearing a filthy black dress and smelling like a putrid corpse, the resurrected Lalaurie is foul-mouthed and contemptuous of the new society in which she finds herself. She especially detests being in proximity to the only black witch among the boarding school residents.

Although *American Horror Story* seems to evidence enlightened racial politics by eventually turning the hateful Lalaurie character into a servant for the black witch, it reproduces familiar and disturbing dynamics. The television show flaunts tortured slaves and showcases a strange and hateful mistress whose intense racism is presented as deviant. The story also incorporates the element of Voodoo so common to popular southern ghost stories that trade on the history of slavery. In the TV show as in the ghost-tour narratives that capitalize on Lalaurie's history, punishment visited upon the bodies of slaves is essential to the story's horrific allure.

A single dramatic exchange between the Lalaurie character and the black female witch character in the show encapsulates the implicit message of the Lalaurie ghost story. Inside the witches' boarding school where Lalaurie is being held captive, Lalaurie and the young black witch face off in an explosive scene. Lalaurie hurls the epithet "Slave!" at the girl, who in turn spits back at her "Bitch!" This scene, which highlights a subjugated racial caste status as well as a cultural critique of unfeminine behavior, distills the fundamental elements of the Lalaurie haunting tale. For the Lalaurie story is at base about abject slaves and unsexed white women; it is a narrative that denies African American agency outside the caricatured realm of Voodoo and demonizes white women outside the bounds of Anglo-feminine respectability. By replaying scenes of brutal black suffering and blaming a single "Creole" woman for the crimes of a whole society, tales of Delphine Lalaurie and her haunted house reanimate antebellum notions of race, gender, ethnic, and power inequities.[42]

The Ghosts of Cities Past

Savannah, Georgia, and New Orleans, Louisiana, jockey for the fame that comes with being deemed the most haunted city in America. While Savannah officially won that title from the American Institute of Parapsychology in 2002, New Orleans stubbornly claims it. Tour guides and authors in both locales tie their towns' hauntedness to a cauldron brew of antiquity, disaster, and senseless death. They regularly cite colonial fires, yellow fever epidemics, and various wars over centuries (Indian wars, the Revolutionary War, and the Civil War) as the main causes of paranormal disturbance. Restless spirits born of disaster glide about the shadowed streets of New Orleans's Vieux Carré and Savannah's stately squares. Both Savannah and New Orleans boast numerous haunted sites and various kinds of ghosts: barmaids in saloons, pirates by the waterfront, victims in the path of fires, or dead children in Catholic school buildings. In each metropolis, though, the dwelling said to be the most haunted is a grand home once occupied by southern elites and their slaves.

"The Haunted House in Royal Street," so named by New Orleans writer George Washington Cable in 1888, was marked for its history of violent slave abuse perpetrated by French Creole slave mistress Madame Lalaurie. The Sorrel-Weed House in Savannah is currently advertised as the most haunted house in that city due to the love triangle gone wrong of patriarch Francis Sorrel, his slave Molly, and his wife Matilda Sorrel. The Lalaurie mansion haunting is an old story, dating back to the late 1800s, while the Sorrel-Weed House haunting is a relatively new, twenty-first-century phenomenon. Despite widely divergent dates of origin for their attached ghost stories, both of these historic sites are tied to commercial ventures that capitalize on representations of the antebellum past, and both houses are seeing a boom in public interest and visits.

The narratives tied to the Sorrel-Weed and Lalaurie homes—told through tours, brochures, books, websites, reality TV shows, social media, and tourist videos—share significant themes in common. A French colonial backdrop connects these stories, which makes the villainous main characters seem especially foreign, exotic, and therefore dangerous to a largely American audience. A core feature of that danger stems from the threat of Voodoo, an African-inspired religion based in the former French colony of Haiti. Both stories also involve the abuse of black slaves, especially women, and a linked moral corruption that affects the entire household. In the Lalaurie and Sorrel homes, white male slaveholders are strangely passive or not what they seem, while white women slaveholders are mentally unsound. There is no "real" white man in the Sorrel-Weed ghost story or in the Lalaurie haunting tale. Delphine Lalaurie reigns over her weak and passive husband, running her abusive household with a maniacal will. Francis Sorrel passes for white when he is actually one-fourth black, wrongfully stealing the spoils of southern society. The absence of proper patriarchs in these tales projects responsibility for violent wrongs onto black men and white women, hence preserving the notions of southern paternalism and white patriarchal morality.

By noting the parallels in these stories, I thought I had in my sights the outlines of a pattern in southern haunted house tours: a French colonial backdrop tinged with a hint of Voodoo, abused black slave women, unstable white mistresses, and nonnormative southern patriarchs. If so, this is a pattern in which no one comes out on top, except, that is, for the white male slaveholder, who never actually appears in these tales but remains, instead, an innocent man somewhere offstage. By sensationalizing the abuses of slavery while protecting white men from blame and by casting doubt on the capacities of white women in positions of authority, both the Lalaurie and Sorrel-Weed ghost stories seem to popularize corrupt ideas about social relations from the past—ideas that should by now be gone with the wind.

3

Chloe and Cleo
Louisiana Plantation Phantoms

Millions of people each year visit plantation homes where guides
blather on about furniture and silverware. As sites, such homes hide the
real purpose of these places, which was to make African Americans toil
under the hot sun for the profit of the rest of the world.
—Edward Baptist, *The Half Has Never Been Told* (2014)

Every respectable plantation has at least one ghost.
—Jill Pascoe, *Louisiana's Haunted Plantations* (2004)

❧

Traveling the Mississippi River Road

The "Historic Plantation Homes" brochure produced by the Baton
Rouge tourism office highlights forty properties along a meandering
stretch of the Mississippi River that spans the state lines of Louisiana
and Mississippi. Iconic abodes of movie set and postcard fame are
all featured here, including the tree-lined Oak Alley Plantation, the
white-columned Nottoway Plantation, and the delicately ornate San
Francisco Plantation. The elaborate brochure describes this collection
of "magnificent" River Road estates as follows:

> Prior to the Civil War, more than half of America's millionaires
> lived between New Orleans and Natchez, their fortunes tied to
> the fertile delta soil of the Mississippi River and its tributaries.
> They lived on plantations ranging in size from hundreds to
> thousands of acres and their homes reflected wealth and an
> opulent way of life—a life that passed with the Civil War. Many of
> these homes were destroyed during and after the War Between
> the States. But many remain restored to their former glory with

care and devotion. Jewels wrought of brick, mortar and stone, they grace the sweeping bends of the Mississippi River and rise up majestically from the verdant fields. . . . You will discover that all these homes have an equal wealth in lore: some romantic, some tragic, some extraordinary, some quaint. As you hear these stories, the day-to-day life of the Old South will come alive in your imagination.[1]

I could pause to comment on how references to fertile rivers and lush green fields have the effect of naturalizing the picture of a luxurious antebellum way of life, or to note how the language of "tragedy" and "romance" almost makes it feel as though the reader should be nostalgic for those bygone days of slavery. But I will resist such criticisms, because the truth is, I clung to this overwrought brochure like a lifeline during my weekend trek along the River Road tourism trail.

I arrived in rural Louisiana on a chilly late December day sheeted with rain. In the West Feliciana Historical Society of the quant historic town of St. Francisville, I was lucky enough to stumble upon the last copy of this state tourism office brochure in the kiosk. I used the pamphlet (complete with map, lists, plantation photos, phone numbers, and a lovely magnolia blossom icon—Louisiana's state flower) in tandem with a book I had read on the plane, *Louisiana's Haunted Plantations*, in order to navigate this elongated chain of widespread plantation sites. Fancy plantation houses, puffed up and pastel-colored like so many wads of cotton candy, dotted the back roads and byways of a 175-mile stretch along and around Interstate 61. In historical museums, gift shops, and cafés along the route, images of these same homes were framed on walls, silk-screened on T-shirts, printed on posters, and emblazoned on mugs. Plantation houses in all of their architectural glory were the belles of the River Road ball, competing for the attention of tourists who came to admire their timeless beauty.

I noticed, as I navigated through the haze and drizzle, that each house seemed to have its own particular style, its own way of standing out from the general plantation pack. Some touted their neoclassical, snow-white porch columns; some emphasized their eighteenth-century age. Some flashed their French Colonial architectural embellishments. Others highlighted their historically accurate gardens. A handful operated as bed-and-breakfasts; a few had southern-style restaurants on the premises. The largest and one of the most famous destinations,

Nottoway Plantation in White Castle (yes, really), Louisiana, is advertised as a full-service resort and hosts a mystery dinner theater. Many of the plantation homes were popular spots for what some couples seem to consider storybook wedding settings. And several of these plantations claimed resident ghosts: the spirits of plantation owners and their sons, ladies dressed in white, ladies dressed in black, Confederate soldiers, unruly pirates, and African American slaves.[2]

It was quite apparent during my journey along the River Road route that traditional plantation tourism was still thriving in the South. Most tours of the homes on the map presented conservative interpretations that emphasized the history and lore of plantation-owning families, the daily lifestyles of elites in the cotton kingdom, and the cultural history of architecture, arts, and antiques. (At Destrehan Plantation, however, my refreshing tour guide, a young African American woman who was fairly new to the job, constantly made critical asides about the punishment of slaves, status of women, and lack of good hygiene at the home, making it nearly impossible for guests to romanticize the plantation.) But even amidst the overall traditionalism of River Road plantation tour scripts, dark tourism was making inroads. Much like historic home and walking tours in Charleston, Savannah, and New Orleans, rural plantation sites were adopting the notion of haunted history in order to boost tourism and diversify visitor experiences. My mission for that dreary long weekend was to visit plantations haunted by slave ghosts on the Louisiana side of the River Road trail. I identified four sites: The Myrtles Plantation (with several enslaved specters and a spiritual portal to boot), Frogmore Plantation (with a house slave ghost), Ormond Plantation (cursed by an angry slave), and Loyd Hall (where a slave nanny was poisoned to death).

I first arranged to spend a night at the elegant Ormond Plantation in Destrehan, Louisiana (near the aforementioned Destrehan Plantation), which is said to carry the curse of an abused slave. However, when I asked the proprietor about the curse, she immediately sought to reassure me. "There is *no* curse," she stressed with upbeat yet insistent encouragement, "just a mystery." My host, a pleasant white woman perhaps in her forties who was busily cleaning up after a wedding party, avoided confirming the story of the supposed wrath of a "brutally disciplined" slave that local author Jill Pascoe had told in her *Louisiana's Haunted Plantations* book.[3] There was, it seemed, a delicate line to be straddled for plantation owners and site managers who sought to capitalize on the dark-tourism trend. Saying a home was haunted or cursed by slaves could get a site included in the many guidebooks and best-of lists that cater to readers with supernatural interests. But overstressing the dark or dangerous nature of a site carried the risk of frightening off traditional plantation home tourists who sought straightforward history and aesthetic enjoyment.

My fellow guests at the Ormond Plantation bed-and-breakfast seemed to fall into the latter category. Over a delicious meal of omelets, fried potatoes, and biscuits prepared by a skillful cook who looked like a long-bearded motorcycle rider, I took in my fellow diners' conversation. Two older white women, both from the South, admired the long dining room and elegant antique furnishings as they plotted their day of River Road plantation tours. "Wouldn't it have been lovely to be served in a room like this back in the olden days?" one of the women asked her friend, who gushed in agreement. They chatted comfortably with the other guests at the table (an older white couple from Ohio and a young white couple from Louisiana) but rarely looked at me. Perhaps the sight of an African American woman enjoying biscuits right alongside them distracted from the fantasy of being served in the "olden days." But elsewhere along the River Road, the fantasy of gracious living supported by a servile, racialized labor force could be amply indulged. A restaurant in the shape of a larger-than-life Mammy figure towered on the roadside along the highway to Natchez. Diners who wished to eat in Mammy's Cupboard would enter the woman's pinkish skirt, which made up the walls of the 1940 structure. Dark-faced Mammy dolls and figurines were for sale in all the gift shops I visited, and copies of the children's book *Little Black Sambo* abounded. (In one shop I counted three different versions of this 1899 British classic. U.S. editions of the book featuring stereotypical images of black "pickaninnies" have been criticized by African American librarians and authors as negative racial portrayals since the 1930s.)[4] Some sites and gift shops included works of African American literature or history among their items, but many did not.

Frogmore Plantation in Ferriday, Louisiana, deserves notice for stocking books on black history (Solomon Northup's *Twelve Years a Slave*), women's history (Catherine Clinton's *The Plantation Mistress*), and Native American history (Robbie Ethridge's *Creek Country*), albeit alongside Mammy paraphernalia and slavery apologia tomes.[5] Frogmore also stood out for its instructive tour of restored and interpreted slave quarters, cotton-production structures, and agricultural

The Myrtles Plantation brochure, Louisiana. This brochure collected by the author in 2013 features The Myrtles Plantation, one among many historic plantations along the Mississippi River Road in Louisiana and Mississippi. The Myrtles is advertised as "One of America's Most Haunted Houses."

implements. My tour guide there, a serious and intrepid woman with no-nonsense brown hair, led me through the grounds in the pouring rain with only a broken umbrella for cover. She asked if I had seen *Twelve Years a Slave*, the movie, which prompted me to ask how close we were to the Louisiana plantations where most of that story had taken place. She told me that Solomon Northup, author of the slave narrative that had been made into a feature film that year, had been held as a slave just over an hour north of Frogmore. While she was eager to talk about Northup, my guide did not even mention the slave ghost that haunts the Frogmore main house, according to plantation owner Lynette Tanner.

This ghost, a house slave seen wearing dark clothing beneath a red apron, appeared to Tanner's daughter soon after the family had begun restoring the property. While Tanner had described the ghostly visit in an interview with Jill Pascoe for the *Haunted Plantations* book, she had apparently not inserted the story into the Frogmore tour, which takes an agricultural angle. Still, Tanner did publicize the ghost story through her interview with Pascoe, securing a place for Frogmore in a popular tome that serves as a guidebook for travels through Louisiana. Tanner's subtle adaptation to the ghost fancy zeitgeist brought to mind my conversations with tour guides in New Orleans and Charleston who said that ghost tourism was a trend that compelled some degree of incorporation by mainstream tours. Sites like Ormond Plantation and Frogmore Plantation seemed to flirt with the notion of haunting, placing ghost stories in printed works or referring to mysterious deaths on their websites but downplaying those stories on location, where they wished to set a different tone. In contrast to the arm's-length strategy evident at Frogmore Plantation, one site along the River Road was not at all shy about its specters. The famously haunted Myrtles Plantation flaunts its ghosts, and I set out to discover how.

The Myrtles Plantation Haunting

When I arrived at The Myrtles Plantation on the cusp of a midwinter evening, buzzards were circling the place. I saw the first dark-winged bird while turning off I-61 into the open gate that fronts the secluded acreage. More of the scavengers, perhaps even twenty, flew overhead as I followed the road through manicured grounds of moss-draped oaks and crepe myrtles. I passed a classical statue, female in form, twisted and gazing at things unseen, and hoped the buzzards were only props, like the resident black cats on the premises that I had read about in a travel writer's essay. The author had described black felines in heat slinking around the buildings and spooking the overnight guests.[6] But the birds were wild, of course, as was my anxiety about staying overnight at The Myrtles. As if my innate hesitation were not enough cause for concern, I had been cautioned to tread carefully by two kindly strangers.

At the Baton Rouge airport, the rental car clerk, a white woman in her sixties, had asked where I was headed and then seemed startled when I told her The Myrtles.

"Are you going for a wedding?" she said.

"To see the house," I answered.

"Are you staying around here?" By "here" she meant the city of Baton Rouge, which was about thirty miles south of the plantation. I confessed that I was staying at The Myrtles, a disclosure met by silence. She looked at me beneath heavily made-up eyelids and a head of curler-coiffed hair. "That one is haunted," she finally said. "I'm scared to go out there."

I took her disclosure as a warning, in the same way that I took the words of the equally interested store clerk in St. Francisville. A charming, pocket-book-sized town with lavishly restored Creole-style cottages, St. Francisville is situated on the Mississippi River in West Feliciana Parish. The Myrtles, also a Creole cottage on a grander scale, hovers just beyond the town's historic district, up a long and meandering road. I was exploring the riverside town and had stopped inside a women's apparel shop when the clerk, a young woman with blonde hair piled into a tousled knot, asked me what I was planning to do in the area. I told her, beginning to feel like a broken record, that I was there to see The Myrtles. She leaned toward me over the glass counter arranged with headbands, dangly earrings, and hair clips and told me that a boy who had stayed at The Myrtles the night before came to town that day with a photo of Chloe, the black woman ghost, on his smart phone. "I saw it myself," the clerk insisted. "It was Chloe through a window. That stuff is true. My mother knows the owners. They used to hear their kids playing with somebody when there was no one there." I asked if she had been there herself. "Yes," she said, "but I would *never* stay overnight."

And yet I was planning to do just that, violating two personal vows that had been firm before I embarked on this peculiar research project: the first not to sleep in a plantation house and the second not to sleep in a haunted house. According to former and present owners, employees, visitors, travel writers, and the local as well as national press, The Myrtles was both. The sensational *National Enquirer* magazine had dubbed the site America's Most Haunted House in the 1980s, and the appellation stuck. Visitors totaling around 40,000 people a year came from around the United States and the world to experience The Myrtles.[7]

David Bradford, a conspirator in the whiskey rebellion of 1794, built The Myrtles Plantation in the late eighteenth century. When

President George Washington cracked down on the armed rebel leaders who were resisting U.S. government taxes, Bradford, a member of that group, fled. After his escape from Pennsylvania, Bradford sought seclusion in the wilds of Spanish Louisiana. He purchased a Spanish land grant and began construction of a small domestic structure, the present-day General's Store, where guests at The Myrtles buy tickets, shop for gifts, and enjoy hearty, home-style breakfasts following overnight stays. Bradford relocated his wife, Elizabeth, and five children to St. Francisville, Louisiana. He had a rustic plantation home built on the grounds, which he called Laurel Grove. After Bradford's death in 1808, Elizabeth legally acquired the property. In 1817, their daughter, Sarah Matilda Bradford, married Clark Woodruff, a lawyer who would become a judge. Both Elizabeth Bradford and Clark Woodruff owned slaves, but the exact number of bondspeople held by each over time is difficult to determine. Elizabeth Bradford (recorded as "Eliza") is listed as having twenty-four slaves in the 1820 U.S. census; Clark Woodruff, her son-in-law, is listed as owning five slaves in that same year.[8] Clark Woodruff later acquired ownership of the plantation from Elizabeth Bradford. The 1830 U.S. census for the Parish of West Feliciana lists ten slaves in possession of Elizabeth Bradford and thirty-three slaves in possession of Clark Woodruff, indicating that Woodruff may have gained ownership of some of the Bradford slaves. Between 1823 and 1824, Sarah Bradford Woodruff died along with two of her children; yellow fever may have been the cause. According to Myrtles chronicler Rebecca Pittman (who does not include detailed footnotes), by 1830 Woodruff owned 4,000 acres and 480 slaves. In 1834 Woodruff sold the plantation to Ruffin Gray Stirling and his wife, Mary Catherine Cobb. The Stirlings, who together owned 173 black men, women, and children ranging in age from infancy to seventy years, sought to turn The Myrtles into their main residence and showplace.[9] They enlarged and embellished the house, orchestrated the planting of myriad crepe myrtle trees, and renamed the plantation The Myrtles. They added the ornate European chandeliers and elaborate floral moldings formed of moss and clay plaster that caused one modern-day guest to say touring The Myrtles was like being on the inside of a wedding cake. After Ruffin Stirling's death in 1854, Mary Cobb Stirling took over the operation of the family plantations. Her daughter, Sarah Mulford Stirling, had married attorney William Winter in 1852, and Mary Cobb requested Winter's help in managing the properties. The family lost the home to debt two years after the close of the Civil War, but Sarah Winter later regained her father's property. Her husband, William Winter, was murdered by an unknown assailant at home in 1871. Theories abound about the possible motives for Winter's dramatic demise, suggesting political conflict in the Reconstruction-era state government or economic motives over ownership of the plantation. Sarah Winter and her mother remained at The Myrtles until their deaths. The Myrtles then passed through the hands of several owners in the twentieth century.[10]

At least three books have been written about The Myrtles: a memoir by former owner Frances Kermeen, a popular history by nonfiction writer Rebecca Pittman, and a forthcoming mystery novel with a Voodoo theme by former lead docent Mark Leonard.[11] While the literature and lore on The Myrtles Plantation is rich with history about the property's several white owners, it conveys virtually nothing about enslaved African American residents. For their stories, we have only the trail of ghosts. This actuality became clear to me during my time at the West Feliciana Historical Society, the museum where I purchased the Mississippi River plantations map that became my lifeline on the trip. A polite elderly woman had offered me assistance as I walked through the shop and adjoining historical exhibits. I had asked if she knew where I could find information about African Americans at The Myrtles and nearby plantations. "Yes, in that book," she had said, pointing me to a title called *The Haunting of Louisiana*.[12] I bought it and found a detailed version of the slave ghost story that I would later hear on the Myrtles Mystery Tour.

The Myrtles main house is an aged two-story cottage just around a bend in the road beyond the plantation entry gates. The structure appears delicate, even dainty, with outstretched porches below and galleries above, all bedecked by ocean-green shutters and decorative iron railings. When I arrived on a rainy late December day, the lot behind the carriage house, a working restaurant, was packed with cars. Groups of guests waited for the next tour, standing in the rain-soaked brick courtyard or sitting in white rocking chairs on the long veranda. I made my way to the General's Store, the oldest building on the plantation that had been the original Bradford dwelling, got my room key, and bought a ticket for that evening's Mystery Tour.

I followed an employee up a steep, narrow staircase, one of two on the back of the house, which led to a set of four upper guest rooms. I swayed as I walked, feeling off balance due to the sharpness of the

The Myrtles Plantation House, St. Francisville. The Myrtles Plantation main house pictured here was the showplace of a Louisiana plantation that ran on the forced labor of over 150 African American slaves. Myrtles Plantation in St. Francisville, Louisiana, March 19, 2005, Wikimedia Commons.

incline. On the landing, the floorboards felt oddly slanted; the doors seemed strangely small for their frames, causing me to feel as though I had been transported into an oversized dollhouse. The employee showed me to the Ruffin Stirling room, where I would be sleeping that night. The room was large and spare, with a few rickety antiques, a romantic framed print of cherubic Victorian children, cut-glass light fixtures atop the fireplace mantel, two locked alcoves to the side of the bed, and cracked and peeling ceiling paint. Heat swooshed erratically through the vent on the ceiling, dispelling the chill from the room and causing the glass beads of the lamps on the mantel to sway. There was an odd, faint smell in the walls and at the windowsills, like old age or mildew. I did not like this room. I left it as soon as possible, went down for dinner in the Carriage House Restaurant (which serves delicious bread pudding), and then bunched up on the long back porch with fellow guests in wait for the Mystery Tour.[13]

There were about thirty of us gathered on that night for the 8:00 P.M. tour, which is mainly taken by overnight guests at the plantation. Most of my fellow tourists were young and white. Among the group were one Latina, a Latino-white mixed-race family with two teenaged boys, one white lesbian couple, and a white family with two school-aged children. Our guide, Mark Leonard, the senior docent at The Myrtles, told stories with a folksy, witty air. He was an older, gray-haired man, unselfconsciously dressed in a white-collared golf shirt and baseball cap. Outside the house he took our tickets, told us there were no phones or photos allowed except in one predesignated spot, and admonished us not to touch the antique furniture. The tour began in the first-floor hallway of the house, a wide-open space with cypress floors, a chandelier, and delicately etched door panes. Leonard told us that although he had never seen a ghost at The Myrtles in the three-plus years that he had been working there, he thought the place was haunted. With hands in pockets, he launched into two contemporary ghost stories about couples who were visited by entities in the Ruffin Stirling room—my room—during their stay at The Myrtles. A ghost hurling the husband's loose change at them startled one couple awake. They barely made it out of the room without being injured. Another couple awoke after a ghost pushed the husband off the bed. The wife scrambled out of the blankets to join him, and as the couple watched, frozen, from the table and chairs at the foot of the bed, they saw a strange shape take form beneath the covers. It was not uncommon, Leonard told our group, for guests to flee The Myrtles in the middle of the night, but, he assured us, no one had ever been seriously hurt, as the spirits here meant no true harm. I was not the only one in our group riveted by Leonard's bizarre stories, grasping my arms more tightly about me and hoping not to feel a cold spot that might indicate, as Leonard had informed us, the presence of a spirit.

Leonard shifted smoothly in his narration from the present to the past, telling us The Myrtles's signature tale, the "legend of Chloe," which he said he believed was "the story of one our ghosts." The legend went as follows: Judge Clark Woodruff was the husband of Sarah Matilda Bradford Woodruff, whose father had founded the plantation. After marrying the young Sarah, Woodruff soon noticed a slave girl on the plantation, thirteen- or fourteen-year-old Chloe. He brought Chloe into the main house to be his concubine. But Chloe had a bad habit of eavesdropping on the judge. He caught her with her ear pressed to the door of the gentlemen's parlor while he was engaged in business one day. As punishment, he had Chloe's left ear cut off and banished her to the plantation kitchen behind the big house. Chloe took to donning a headwrap to hide her deformity and wore only one earring on her remaining ear. She could not stand her state of exile and wished to get back into the Woodruff household, so she concocted a plan. She would bake a birthday cake for the judge's twin daughters and spike it with the poisonous leaves of the oleander plant. The cake would sicken the girls, but Chloe would nurse them back to health, and all would be forgiven. Chloe's plan went terribly awry, however. The Judge' s wife and twin daughters died from the toxic cake. A terrified Chloe ran to the slave quarters, seeking asylum, but her fellow slaves revealed her whereabouts to the judge and made her confess. The judge in turn forced the other slaves to hang Chloe. Afterward the slaves dumped her body into the depths of the Mississippi River. Due to her violent death and improper burial, Chloe haunts the big house and grounds of The Myrtles today.

After telling the story of Chloe, Leonard led our tour group into the French Bedroom, decorated in gold-leafed furnishings original to the house, and recounted the story of an actress who had stayed in that room. The actress was on the grounds to play Chloe in a performance, and she was dressed up like the slave woman. In the dark of night, the actress saw a green mist floating toward her, the ghost of Chloe. In a panic, the actress ran and bumped her head hard on a locked door, bloodying herself. She was the only person who had ever been seriously injured as the result of an encounter with a Myrtles ghost.

In this same French Bedroom, Leonard told us the story of Cleo, a Voodoo priestess who had lived as a slave on the nearby Solitude Plantation. He said that in the 1840s, the Stirling family, who had bought the place from Judge Woodruff, had a child suffering from yellow fever. Ruffin Stirling was desperate to save his child's life and so requested the services of Cleo despite his distaste for Voodoo and his fear that the slave religion could foment rebellion. Cleo was left to work her ritual magic on the child in the nursery (the present-day Ruffin Stirling room). Sounds of drums and mysterious chants echoed through the house that night. Finally, Cleo emerged and proclaimed the girl healed. Ruffin Stirling was so grateful that he allowed Cleo, a lowly slave, to sleep in his wife's day room, the golden-leafed lady's chamber where our tour group was then standing. By dawn, however, Stirling discovered that his daughter had passed away. Stirling shouted for the overseer, and together they dragged the sleeping Cleo from the gilded room and into the front yard of The Myrtles, where they strung her up on an oak tree, asphyxiating her. In recent years, a film producer who stayed in the

French Bedroom saw Cleo hanging from the ceiling, as vividly as "a real lynching." Due to concerns about the potency of the spiritual presence there, the staff at The Myrtles no longer allows guests to sleep in the French Bedroom. Our tour guide was a practiced storyteller who knew the importance of pacing in the rendering of events. By the time he told the story of a phantom Cleo hanging from a lynch mob's spectral noose, those of us gathered in the room had gone still.

Leonard then led our group out of the French Bedroom and into the hallway where The Myrtles's famous haunted mirror hangs in a prominent position. This mirror contains dark shadows that are said to be the imprinted spirits of the dead wife and children of Judge Woodruff. Photos of the haunted mirror are encouraged, as are photos of the home's exterior and grounds. (A number of guests have reported capturing the image of Chloe outside. Hester Eby, the longest-serving employee at The Myrtles and an African American woman, recalled a photograph taken by a guest that pictured a hazy image of Chloe hanging dead from a tree.)[14] My fellow tourists and I eagerly raised our cameras, snapping away at the haunted mirror. Three among us took this brief moment of permitted electronics use to turn on ghost radar equipment and scan the space. One of the three admitted that her equipment was borrowed from a coworker who insisted that she bring it if she was coming to The Myrtles. The other two, a couple, said that tracking ghosts was the whole point of being here and asked our guide if they could switch to a more haunted room for their overnight stay.

Leonard led us through the house, which felt somber to me despite its bright-colored walls, artful floral moldings, and plaster ceiling medallions. Leonard pointed to an empty spot in the middle of the gentlemen's parlor that many psychics say is a spiritual portal, a doorway where spirits pass from this world to the next. This portal pre-dated the structure of the house and is said to have been connected to the prior residence of Tunica Indians who dwelled here before the arrival of the French and Spanish. Leonard showed us, at the end of the tour, a grainy photograph that the current homeowner, Teeta Moss, had taken in 1992. The picture featured the carriage house and a faint image of a woman's form standing next to an exterior wall: it was Chloe, in a long, old-fashioned work dress, caught on film. On top of the building, fainter still, were two squatting shadows: the children that Chloe had inadvertently murdered with her poisonous birthday cake. The characters of Chloe and Cleo, two black slave women, were the most vividly rendered of the panoply of Myrtles ghosts that Leonard described to us. Other specters that are said to haunt the place are the two children killed by Chloe; the child lost to yellow fever; William Winter, a later owner of the plantation who was shot by a cloaked stranger; Winter's wife, Sarah, dressed in black and mourning her husband; a polite Confederate soldier who frequents the home; and a 1920s caretaker who wanders the grounds, sometimes telling tourists that the place is closed.

After the tour I stayed behind, not wanting to return to my eerie upstairs bedroom, the former nursery and so-called scene of Cleo's Voodoo ritual as well as the ghostly attacks on previous guests that we had heard about at the start of the tour. I asked Leonard if he believed the place was haunted, if he *really* believed. "Yes, unequivocally," he said. "I feel the spirits' presence. . . . But maybe they are not ghosts in the way that we tend to think of ghosts. Maybe they are actually time wrinkles." By "time wrinkle" Leonard meant a stuck spot in the temporal zone, a place of continual return, something like an automatic repeat button on a paranormal digital recorder. If this were the case, Leonard surmised, then the historical figures of The Myrtles were not going through painful moments perpetually. He really could not see a God putting people through that, Leonard said. According to his theory, Cleo's spirit was not being hanged again and again at the scene of her death in the 1840s. It just seemed as though she was being hanged to those who saw her ghost because of a sort of metaphysical TiVo machine. But then what was determining which scenes were chosen for replay at The Myrtles? I did not ask him this question. But it seemed to me that the confluence of consumer demand and vendor supply was producing an emphasis on scenes of slavery, which were also, to borrow the language of literary critic Saidiya Hartman, "scenes of subjection"—representations of brutality and submission rendered as spectacle.[15]

The stories of Chloe and Cleo told on the Myrtles Mystery Tour are fundamentally stories of violence against black women—sexual violence, physical violence, and ideological violence. Chloe's sexual submission to a male slaveholder twice her age is presented not only as mundane but also as Chloe's preferred situation. After being removed from the big house by the man who ordered her torture, she schemes to get back into close proximity to him. Cleo's practice of Voodoo is an element of her story that adds exoticism and Louisiana local flavor to The Myrtles lore. The practice of her faith (drums, chants) is rendered as primitively African, culturally impenetrable, and spiritually dangerous.

Her murder is eroticized, as two white men drag her from the gold-leafed bed and murder her in the yard. Both Chloe and Cleo are linked, either directly or indirectly, to the deaths of innocent white children, thus subtly shading them with a measure of guilt in their own demise and lessening the perceived moral wrong of their killings.

The stories of Chloe and Cleo presented in The Myrtles Mystery Tour have been taken up and embellished by writers and visitors to the house in print and online. Chloe is the particular entity of focus and the favorite spirit among these writers, many of whom claim to have encountered her. As a ghost, Chloe accrues characteristics that thicken her subjection in cultural memory. She is imagined as alternately embodying two of this nation's most prominent negative stereotypes of African American women: the Jezebel and the Mammy. The Jezebel type, named for a North African woman of ill repute in the Bible, is the sexually insatiable, morally impure, manipulative black slave woman who tempts men into her bed, threatening the sanctity of the white family. As numerous scholars of black women's history have demonstrated, the Jezebel figure has its origins in seventeenth- and eighteenth-century European male travelers' narratives about Africa in which African women featured prominently. Authors of these narratives commented on what they interpreted as African women's lewd state of undress, lack of pain in childbirth, "monstrous" physical characteristics (such as overly long breasts and large buttocks), and loose sexual practices (including the charge of sexual relations with orangutans). These reportedly negative gender and sex characteristics were bundled into an idea of racial difference, an idea of inferior "blackness" versus superior "whiteness," that was only then taking shape in the modern European world. Black women and the peoples produced out of their animalistic wombs were seen as naturally inferior. Once African women were transported across the Atlantic Ocean and forced into inhumane conditions of enslavement, they appeared even more to white observers to be lacking in goodness, modesty, and chastity. Rather than seeing black women as victims of a system that stole their personal right to bodily integrity, white slaveholding society labeled black women as Jezebels, manipulative sexual temptresses who brought on and deserved their fate.[16]

Chloe, the young girl on Judge Woodruff's plantation (said by various tour guides to be as old as fourteen and as young as twelve), is a classic Jezebel type. She catches the judge's eye, wins a place in his household, desires to stay in his home, and thus concocts a scheme that threatens the white mistress and children of the estate. Stories told by people who have seen Chloe's ghost note her attractiveness and the competitive tension between Chloe and her mistress, Sarah Woodruff. Former owner of The Myrtles Frances Kermeen published the first stories of Chloe ghost sightings in her memoir *The Myrtles Plantation: The True Story of America's Most Haunted House* (2005). In this narrative psychodrama of Kermeen's seduction by the haunted house in the 1980s and the resulting ruin of her marriage, Kermeen encounters numerous spirits. Kermeen and her husband Jim were the first Myrtles owners to turn the plantation into a business, a bed-and-breakfast that hosted a mystery dinner theater and offered tours. In her memoir, Kermeen recounts the stories of an overnight guest who sees the slave ghost Chloe, writing, "She found a mulatto slave dressed in a green frock with a green turban wrapped around her head whimpering in the corner. . . . The slave told her that her name was Chloe and that she had just learned that her father was white." Kermeen also mentions a psychic who saw "a beautiful young slave girl in the green turban." By the end of the memoir, Kermeen has become so possessed by The Myrtles and its spirits that she is completely identified with the antebellum mistress, Sarah Woodruff. In the final chapter of the book, Kermeen writes in the voice of a plantation mistress, imagining herself waking up to the sounds of "voodoo drums faintly in the distance" and "house servants . . . humming as they went about their daily tasks." Kermeen reveals "the whisperings behind her back" that she constantly hears about her husband "carrying on with one of the slaves." Kermeen knows which slave it is because of revealing eye contact between the two women, and she realizes on the last page of the book that the slave has poisoned her cup of tea in a bid to secure Kermeen's husband. Kermeen then snaps out of this historical fantasy brought on by the haunted house and realizes that she must abandon The Myrtles. She moves back to California, where she will be safe from the home's evil power.[17]

In *The Haunting of Louisiana*, the book that was recommended to me at the local historical society as a source for African American history, the author includes several stories featuring Chloe's ghost. One of those stories is about a couple from New Orleans who kept hearing strange music and finding a rumpled bed in their room. Author Barbara Sillery reports that "speculation abounds that this room is a battleground between the spirit of Chloe, who leaves her imprint on the bed in defiance of her former mistress, and the fastidious Sara

Woodruff, who struggles to maintain order." In this anecdote, the battle over the bed sheets between Chloe and Sarah can be interpreted as a symbolic struggle over the intimate space of the marriage bed and Judge Clark Woodruff's affections. Chloe is presented as being actively engaged in this battle, as fighting for her place in the house and bedroom. Sillery also recounts the charge often made by The Myrtles tour guides and guests that "the conniving Chloe" is a thief who steals earrings from women to adorn her single ear and snatches hair ribbons from little girls in an attempt to get back at the Woodruff daughters for eating too much poisoned birthday cake. The Chloe-as-thief stories can be interpreted as further proof of her competition with white women, as she attempts to steal the accoutrements of their femininity for herself. Chloe emerges in these contemporary representations as a manipulative, immoral slave girl who wants what rightfully belongs to the mistress: a sexual relationship with her master.[18]

The ugly side of Chloe's eroticized image represents the threat to white society posed by the supposedly predatory sexuality of black women, but some Myrtles guests also view Chloe's story as romantic. As one of The Myrtles tour guides who wants to remain anonymous explained to me in an interview, Chloe has numerous "fans," many of them young girls who see Chloe as a sort of "Disney Princess" figure. These girls come on the tour and listen to Chloe's tale with "starry eyes." Her move into the big plantation house to become the lover of the master is viewed as redemption of her prior lowly state to these girls, and her ouster to the kitchen is viewed as a tragic downfall. If Chloe's were a real Disney Princess story, the couple should reunite in the end and live happily ever after, but perhaps these young tourists see the presence of Chloe's ghost as a kind of reunion between Chloe and the house, if not between Chloe and the man she supposedly loved. How parents can look on while their daughters respond in this way to such a gruesome story is inexplicable, the tour guide told me. I agreed and could not help but recall one of my visits to The Myrtles, during which a Girl Scout troop played in the courtyard while waiting to take the tour.

Chloe is thus seen by many who encounter her story as the hypersexual Jezebel of the slavery era and also as a "tragic mulatta," the recurring figure in American literature of the beautiful mixed-race black woman who cannot find happiness because she is thwarted by a white lover and trapped by her racial designation. The tragic mulatta is the refined, romanticized cousin of Jezebel portrayed as a light-skinned woman with Christian ideals, domestic aspirations, and an appearance that is attractive to white men because of her physical closeness to the white ideal of female beauty. Tainted by her sexual relations with white men outside wedlock, the tragic mulatta is nevertheless a figure of pathos, a woman wronged by her circumstances as well as personal weakness.[19]

The figure of Chloe is plastic enough that she also appears to many as a stereotypical Mammy, an imaginative figment of the antebellum period. The Mammy was the ideological counterpoint to the Jezebel, a black woman who served the white family rather than undermining it. Often portrayed as dark-skinned, portly, and older in age, the Mammy managed the white household with skill and loved the white mistress's children as her own. Her supreme charge in life, the charge that she gladly answered, was to care for the white family, suppressing her own needs and the needs of her black children. As scholarship on black women's history shows, the Mammy myth was called into discursive being by defenders of slavery in the 1830s who sought to challenge abolitionist critiques of the sexual abuse of slave women. Mammy's image was embellished by memoirs of slaveholders' children published during the Civil War as well as by tributes to her memory in the late 1800s and early 1900s in the Aunt Jemima pancake-mix brand and plans for a national Mammy memorial spurred by the Daughters of the Confederacy. Even the restaurant noted at the start of this chapter, Mammy's Cupboard on Interstate 61, is part of the southern tradition of what American studies scholar Micki McElya has called "clinging to Mammy."[20]

Sightings of a Mammylike Chloe were first published, again, in Frances Kermeen's memoir. Kermeen recounts her personal encounter with a "woman dressed in a long, flowing, dark green gown, holding a round tin with a candle in it. . . . Her face was dark and very square, and a green turban was wrapped around her head, concealing her hair." When Kermeen summons her courage to ask the former owner of The Myrtles about this apparition, he explains that the slave woman ghost "is seen most often at night, in her green dressing gown and turban. She goes from room to room, carrying her night-candle, checking to be sure that everyone is safe and warm." Kermeen also recounts the story of a guest who saw Chloe and described her as "a large, homely woman with a very square jaw," noting that this image did not match other accounts of the slave woman ghost as light-skinned and pretty. In the near-decade since the publication of Kermeen's memoir, tourists at The Myrtles have often declared in interviews and on websites that Chloe the ghost has a habit of floating about and tucking people in at night. This version of Chloe—the dark-skinned domestic—is still on the job a century and a half after the Civil War, making sure that residents in The Myrtles big house are comfortable.[21]

Safety and comfort may well be what Chloe and plantation ghost tourism writ large are all about in the end. Tourists of the southern region can visit these places and step into fantasy scenes with which they are intimately familiar as participants in American national memory and culture. This is the scene of the rural plantation, idyllic and paternal, where jolly, dark, and, notably, female servants tend to a person's every need: the need for care, the need for comfort, the need for romance, and the need to know that the racial threat—endemic to the plantation where black slaves are held against their will—is fully contained. Containment is key to Chloe's story. Although the tale presents a black woman who takes radical action by daring to poison her owners' family, it also blunts the impact of this threat. Chloe the conniving young temptress was put to death, and her lingering ghost is harmless, reduced to stealing earrings at her worst and providing turndown service at her best. The memory of racial injustice that lurks behind this ghost story is ultimately overshadowed by representations of Chloe as a slave who wished to be the sexual servant of her owner and as a "pesky" but ultimately benign spirit of the dead.[22]

To some contemporary tourists, the Jezebel figure has an allure as the embodiment of black women's dangerous yet enticing eroticism. To others, the Mammy figure has an allure as the soothing black female caretaker, the woman who makes delicious pancakes and doles out enveloping hugs, the succor of the white family. It is convenient, therefore, and not at all surprising, that Chloe has been rendered both ways. Some Myrtles enthusiasts see Chloe as mixed-raced, young, and lovely. Others see her as dark-skinned, older, and heavy. All, I will argue, are extracting something they desire, something reinforcing, from Chloe's popular story. Chloe, the malleable black slave woman ghost, can appear as any visitor's fantasy.

Cleo is secondary to Chloe when it comes to Myrtles ghostly lore, but she is beginning to gain notoriety. Cleo represents the exoticization of black religious practices at The Myrtles and in broader American society. Her most important and indeed only memorable characteristic is her status as a practitioner of Voodoo, which every good slave ghost story apparently requires. (Recall the practice of Voodoo by Savannah slaveholder Francis Sorrel and the conscription of "Voodoo queen" Marie Laveau into the story of Madame Delphine Lalaurie.) And more than a mere adherent of that faith, Cleo is a priestess, like Marie Laveau and the character Minerva in the book that put Savannah on the tourism map.[23] Voodoo lends an exotic quality to these stories, calling to mind the notion of the African primitive. Voodoo also portends spiritual danger for non-adherents who see the religion as strange and dangerous, thereby enhancing the taboo-breaking, fear-inspiring elements of dark tourism. Even Frances Kermeen, whose memoir fixates mainly on the threat of the slave woman temptress, finds a way to interweave the theme of Voodoo into her narrative. Kermeen begins her memoir by recounting a trip to Haiti during which she and her then boyfriend witnessed a "wild and uninhibited" Voodoo ritual. Kermeen relates that she snapped a photograph of the "voodoo warriors" and that they in turn put a curse on her. It is after this encounter that Kermeen stumbles upon the lovely Myrtles Plantation and is so entranced that she feels compelled to purchase it. All of the terrible events that unfold for Kermeen during the decade that she lived in the "evil" house and operated it as a bed-and-breakfast—the death of her beloved dog and of a good friend, and the sexual treachery of her husband—begin with that curse in Haiti.[24]

The Voodoo priestess (sometimes referred to as a Voodoo queen) is another recurring stereotype of African American women that receives less attention than the Jezebel and Mammy in scholarly literature. (Notice the use of the word "queen" as an ironic pejorative in stereotypes that are meant to belittle black women, as in "welfare queen.") Together, Chloe and Cleo come close to embodying the pantheon of what black feminist theorist Patricia Hill Collins has called "controlling images of black womanhood."[25] Chloe wears two faces as both Jezebel and Mammy. Cleo, in turn, is the Voodoo priestess. These two ghosts, Chloe and Cleo (with strikingly similar names), are so closely related in the mythology of black womanhood that they are often confused for each other.[26]

The Life of a Slave Girl

Chloe the girl as well as the ghost appears in these stories as conniving, dishonest, ineffectual, and desirous of a relationship with her master. But what was the actual experience of enslaved black women on rural plantations? Little can be gleaned from The Myrtles Mystery Tour, which distorts the historical reality of African American women's relations with men of the slaveholding class. We know from secondary historical literature that Mississippi River Delta plantations in the era of cotton's heyday (especially during the decades before the Civil War) were places of extreme brutality and deprivation for slaves. Historian Walter Johnson has examined how the plantation, policed by white men on horseback and ferocious attack dogs, was a "carceral landscape," a space of imprisonment for people of African descent. Slaves in these literal labor camps were locked in by a series of swampy waterways and dangerous wild animals, by an increasingly flattened natural world where forests were continually being cleared so there were few hiding places, by a network of slaveholders in cahoots to maintain a harsh racial order, and by the constant threat of violent punishment and familial separation. In addition, slaves had meager material resources. Their homes were small and crowded shacks that provided minimal protection from the elements. Their clothing was cheap, thin, and worn, and many labored with no shoes. Enslaved residents of Louisiana plantations were often hungry, desperate to supplement the meager rations provided by their owners. They were always subject to brutal, often random acts of violence, both as victims and as witnesses, in an environment that can only be described as a vast agrarian torture chamber.[27]

Enslaved black women on plantations were particularly vulnerable. Historians of black women in slavery have detailed the pervasiveness of sexual coercion and rape in a system that not only offered no legal protection for black women but also rewarded masters economically for forced sex and impregnation that resulted in the growth of the slave population. Black women had no right to the privacy of their bodies and were stripped and handled on auction blocks by sellers and buyers alike. Black women were subjected to the sexual advances and assaults of white men around them: their owners, their owners' sons and other relatives, men to whom they might be rented out, overseers, and slave patrollers. They were also paired by their owners with enslaved men and ordered to work as breeders, that is, to engage in intercourse to produce black children, future laborers for the owner's unpaid workforce. Some African American women did choose to engage in short- or long-term sexual relations with white men, but their actions must be seen within a context of widespread sexual exploitation and coercion and of extremely limited options. These women may have hoped to secure freedom for themselves or their children; to improve their material conditions in the form of better living quarters, more food, and nicer clothing; or to protect themselves from other threats such as being sold away from family and friends. A minority of slave women were successful in their quest. However, this kind of choice was a gamble, as many black women who slept with white men were not able, in the end, to achieve free status or protection from sale or violence.

Firsthand accounts in the form of slave narratives are an essential source for learning about life in slavery. In her classic narrative *Incidents in the Life of a Slave Girl*, North Carolinian Harriet Jacobs details the crushing emotional impact of continual sexual harassment and the threat of rape. In a piercing commentary on plantation morality, she observes the corrupt dynamic among masters, mistresses, and slave women: "Even the little child who is accustomed to wait on her mistress and her children, will learn, before she is twelve years old, why it is that her mistress hates such and such a one among the slaves. Perhaps the child's own mother is among the hated ones. She listens to violent outbreaks of jealous passion, and cannot help understanding what is the cause. She will become prematurely knowing in evil things. Soon she will learn to tremble when she hears her master's footfall. . . . If God has bestowed beauty on her, it will prove her greatest curse."[28]

Jacobs lays bare the abuses that fester in a system that guarantees the unfettered power of one group, white men, over another, black women. Jacobs was only fifteen when her master began to stalk her, approximately the same age as Chloe in the Myrtles story. Jacobs wrote about her master as if he were a demon "whose restless, craving vicious nature roved about at night, seeking whom to devour," and she revealed that "he told me I was made for his use, made to obey his command in *every* thing."[29] Rather than scheming to get closer to her sadistic master like Chloe of Myrtles lore, Jacobs concocts a desperate plan to evade him, eventually accepting another white man as a lover. This was not the sexual life that Jacobs had wanted. In fact, she was in love with a free black man. This was, instead, the sexual life that she chose among restrictive and damaging options; she could either be pushed into sex with her master or submit to sex with another white man whose whiteness and class status could shield her from her master's reach. Jacobs noted, in her astute discussion of these racial-sexual dynamics, that living in a town like Edenton, North Carolina, offered her some slim measure of protection from her master. The proximity of his neighbors, business associates, church members, and clients (he was a medical doctor) meant that he was less likely to risk an outright attack on Jacobs that would incur the disapproval of peers. The moral code of southern society dictated that white men must appear to respect their marriage vows and maintain racial purity by refraining from sexual relations with blacks. However, the all-too-common violation of both these tenets was often ignored as long as the white men in question kept their relations with black women semisecret. Jacobs realized that if she had been living on a rural plantation where white households were far apart and social oversight was weaker, her master would likely have forced himself upon her.[30] Chloe of the Myrtles story *did* live on a remote plantation and thus would have had very little chance of escaping Judge Woodruff's advances. As a girl brought into the big house to sexually serve her master, Chloe was living Harriet Jacobs's nightmare. Moreover, as a slave on a plantation in the Mississippi Delta, she was located in a region that slaves in the Upper South and Southeast feared for its extreme conditions and cruelty, as captured in the foreboding yet familiar phrase "sold down the river."

Historical Louisiana is often viewed as a place where interracial relationships were more frequent and more socially acceptable. This perception stems from the state's layered colonial history of French and Spanish jurisdiction, its sizable population of free people of color, and its cultural system of informal marriage between women of color and white men known as "placage."[31] However, scholarship on sex and race in Louisiana has demonstrated the physical and emotional exposure and legal vulnerability of black women even in a context of pliable social expectations around interracial sex and mixed-race families. Gwendolyn Midlo Hall, co-creator of the Louisiana Slavery Database, stresses that "while nonwhite concubines and mixed-race offspring of white men were most likely treated with more consideration in colonial Louisiana than elsewhere in the United States, at the same time brutality toward slave women was probably unmatched." Hall describes an example from the 1780s that personalizes the many cases of abuse. In the 1780s a French colonist named Jacques Ozenne kept his "Mulatresse" Babet naked, forced her to wear a metal bit in her mouth to prevent the intake of food, and lashed her entire body. This brutal treatment led to Babet's death.[32] In colonial and early Louisiana, black enslaved women who coupled with white men lacked the legal protections and social regard of marriage. Their racialized status as black and caste status as slaves meant that their white sex partners could physically abuse them with impunity. They could be sold by their owners, as could their children. And even if these women were born free or acquired freedom for themselves and their children, they would face strict limitations on inheritance in a French and, later, Spanish society that policed the line between people of color and whites by ensuring that whites had legalized economic advantages. As historian Jennifer Spear explains about sexual relationships in early New Orleans: "As elsewhere in the Americas, most were exploitative. Using coercive sex to subordinate women of color, Euro-American men violently reinforced the sexual, gendered, and racial orders of colonial societies."[33]

There are, of course, examples of long-term and by all evidence caring relationships between black women and white men in Louisiana as well as elsewhere in the slaveholding South. However, it is imperative for us to remember that these relationships were the outliers, not the norm, and that they were formed in a social and legal context that drastically limited black women's right to choose. Black women's basic sexual condition in the slave society of Louisiana and across the South was one of vulnerability and coercion.[34] The mechanical technology that led to the nineteenth-century boom in cotton enabled a surge in the importation of slaves from the Upper South. Many of these individuals were women who would wind up on Mississippi River plantations, where they would perform backbreaking agricultural labor and spirit-killing sexual labor. As historian Diana Williams bluntly puts it in her work on race and domestic partnerships in nineteenth-century Louisiana, Louisiana culture constructed "black women's bodies as receptacles for free sex."[35] Being a slave woman on a plantation, even in Louisiana, was no Disney fairytale. This blatant fact makes it alarming that The Myrtles's legend of Chloe could be viewed as an appealing and enjoyable tourist attraction.

It is even more alarming to consider that Chloe is not a historical figure but is instead a fictional character created in the late twentieth century. Similarly to Molly, the slave ghost in Savannah's Sorrel-Weed House, Chloe has no traceable life in the historical record. There is no written or reliable oral indication that she ever existed, which means that her selection by Judge Woodruff as a child sex slave, the torture she endured in the loss of her ear, and her murder at the hands of fellow slaves is all invention.[36] While there is no denying that enslaved girls and women endured horrific circumstances, there is no indication that The Myrtles stories are intended to inform visitors about this historical injustice. Rather, the stories of Chloe and the equally untraceable Cleo trivialize the experience of African American women by ignoring the bleakness of the plantation setting for slaves, caricaturing social relations between male masters and female slaves, and rendering vigilante murders as spectacle. The life of Chloe is what cultural critic Daniel Boorstin has called a pseudo-event, a manufactured happening for which the "relation to the underlying reality of the situation is ambiguous." Pseudo-events are particularly attractive to tourists, Boorstin argues, who want to experience reproductions that meet familiar expectations and are at the same time exciting and strange.[37] Chloe's story satisfies expectations about the shadow side of the plantation setting while at the same time undercutting any serious analysis of the power dynamics therein. Tourists at The Myrtles can therefore flirt with the danger of racial and sexual taboos while never having to really think about human subjection, the corruption of power, and their own voyeuristic complicity in the reproduction of plantation culture scripts. They can, shall we say, have their poisonous oleander cake and eat it too.[38]

Selling Slavery: Haunted Plantation Kitsch at The Myrtles

The Myrtles Plantation seems to have inspired the imagination of visitors with notions of the supernatural since at least the 1940s. A Louisiana state tourism guide from 1941 allows that "several ghost stories are centered on The Myrtles." One of these stories is about "a French lady in a green bonnet," while the other focuses on "the ghost of an infant." The 1945 Louisiana WPA project collection of folktales, *Gumbo Ya-Ya*, describes the Myrtles as having "a lovable specter in the person of a little old French lady in a faded green bonnet, who tiptoes through the rooms at night, evidently searching for someone."[39] A 1961 book of photographs called *Ghosts along the Mississippi: The Magic of the Old Houses of Louisiana*, by Clarence John Laughlin, also includes The Myrtles's lady ghost. In this work of "poetic" photographs that capture old houses in strange and eerie light beneath superimposed images of ghostly figures, Laughlin includes one plate on The Myrtles titled "The Dark Lady." The house, he writes, was associated with "a number of ghost stories," including the wail of a dead baby and the visage of "an old French lady" who searches the rooms for someone in an endless quest by lifting mosquito nettings.[40]

In the 1960s, the same decade when Laughlin's widely exhibited photographs were published as a book, the lore of the Myrtles ghosts began to spread. Oklahoma transplant Marjorie Munson purchased the home and reported hearing stories of a French female ghost that had been "handed down from generation to generation of owners of The Myrtles plantation." The dominant ghost story featured the same wandering French woman represented in gauzy form in Laughlin's photograph. She was sometimes white in the story and sometimes a "French-mulatta" governess wearing a green beret. Munson, who told a writer for the *Baton Rouge Morning Advocate* newspaper that she had "never seen a ghost here" herself, recounted the ghost stories about the French woman and repeated strange accounts of doors unlocking on their own and the appearance of little girl ghosts as told to her by houseguests. Inspired by the story of "the French woman's ghost," Munson wrote lyrics in tribute to the spirit, titled "The Green Beret." It was her desire to set those lyrics to music that led her to seek out composer Dolar Michaud, whom she soon married. Together, the couple set out to restore the old plantation house and transform it into a regional cultural center. They founded the Feliciana Music Festival that continues today and housed an art gallery in the second story of the domicile. Was The Myrtles really haunted? Marjorie Munson Michaud and Dolar Michaud equivocated in their newspaper interview. Whether or not one saw a ghost "all depends upon the individual—his personality, his attunement to extra-sensory perception," the couple said. The 1960 *Morning Advocate* story about their restoration and cultural efforts seems to have been the first to publicize the notion of ghostly entities at The Myrtles. Most revealing for our purposes about The Myrtles's public spectral past is the telling detail that the primary ghost of the original stories does not appear to have been a slave and was only sometimes figured as mixed-race. Early Myrtles ghosts were usually white French women, racially unmarked babies (who we can assume were also white), and white female children.[41]

It was not until the 1980s, when new owner Frances Kermeen turned the plantation into a full-scale bed-and-breakfast business, that black slave ghosts became a regular presence at the house. It stands to reason that during the 1960s, when civil rights activism was at its height, black ghosts of the South would not have been especially alluring to white vacationers. In the post–civil rights Regan era of conservative economics and politics, perhaps the notion of black ghosts became of interest precisely because they were both discomforting and somehow quaintly comfortable. Frances Kermeen's memoir is the first work of any kind of which I am aware to record the presence of Chloe, the slave woman ghost. According to a Myrtles tour guide who wished to remain

Chloe doll for sale at The Myrtles Plantation. This cloth doll representing Chloe the slave ghost was for sale at The Myrtles Plantation gift shop known as the General's Store. The photo pictures the doll lying on the bed of the haunted Ruffin Stirling room, where the author stayed overnight. Photo by the author, 2013.

anonymous, notes from Kermeen's 1980s house tour scripts included the stories of Chloe and other ghosts. So it would seem that former owner Frances Kermeen originated the tale of Chloe and the notion of Voodoo influence at The Myrtles. By all indications, the current owners of the plantation, John and Teeta Moss, have reproduced, multiplied, and expertly marketed the slave ghost stories first publicized by Kermeen. In the 1980s, Kermeen garnered national press coverage for The Myrtles. In recent years the house, and Chloe's story in particular, has been featured by numerous newspaper articles and television shows, including *National Geographic Explorer*, the *Travel Channel*, the *Oprah Winfrey Show*, and *Ghost Hunters*.

This publicity, as well as online videos, posts, and websites created by Myrtles fans and skeptics alike, spread Chloe's notoriety. On one Myrtles tour that I took, the vivacious young woman guide told the crowd she was about to tell the story of The Myrtles's most famous ghost. She asked if the group knew whom she meant, and most people shouted back "Chloe!" Visitors to The Myrtles can even buy material versions of Chloe to take home with them. The photographic image of Chloe's apparition standing by the carriage house is reproduced on Myrtles postcards, and cloth dolls in her imagined likeness are available for sale at The Myrtles gift shop. Chloe the doll has black fabric skin, green eyes, and bright red lips; she wears a turban, an apron, and one gold hoop earring. She also has attached to her long white skirt a personal note from the doll maker, who writes that after encountering Chloe's ghost, she wanted to "keep her memory alive" in the form of this "homemade Louisiana Primitive" (cost: $18.50). Beyond the gift shop, at the Carriage House Restaurant on the plantation, diners can enjoy a specialty drink in tribute to the murdered slave woman: Chloe's Bloody Mary. Although Cleo dolls are not for sale in the gift store (yet), consumables caricaturing Cleo's supposed religious practice are. Guests can find spicy Zapp's Voodoo potato chips as well as Watchover Voodoo dolls on racks that stand beside Myrtles T-shirts, books and videos on Louisiana hauntings, southern recipe mixes, artsy knickknacks, and glass fleur-de-lis pendants. (The little-known fact that the fleur-de-lis symbol was used in the French colonial era to brand slaves for theft makes even this last seemingly harmless keepsake symbolically disturbing.)[42] Merchandise available at The Myrtles reproduces and amplifies the caricatured nature of the slave ghost stories told on the tours and in books, creating an overproduced, lighthearted, commercialized effect that we might call haunted plantation kitsch. "Kitsch," a German term that refers to cheapened goods in a mass commercial culture, is an element of dark-touristic enterprise that works to contain the serious implications of historic sites. By purchasing cute and affordable items as mementos, tourism scholars Richard Sharpley and Philip Stone theorize, travelers can reduce "the political complexity of a macabre event to simplified notions of tragedy." Kitsch objects taken home by the tourist, like stuffed bears, figurines, and slave ghost dolls, "inoculate" visitors against genuine emotion and weighty contemplation by "rendering death and disaster into something else that is comfortable and safe to deal with."[43] The objectification of Chloe as a girl, a ghost, and finally a doll, along with the exoticization of Cleo as a Voodoo priestess, occurs across multiple dimensions of The Myrtles experience, from the tour itself to the items for sale to the afterlife of tourist visits characterized by the circulation of photos and testimonials online.

Chloe's Return: From Plantation Kitsch to Plantation Camp

Halloween is the busy season at The Myrtles, a time when tour groups mushroom in size and booking a room in the main house is close to impossible. I barely secured lodging in Live Oak Cabin, one of four modern cabins built behind the old plantation house, when I called two months in advance. I was apprehensive about this October visit, expecting to hear disturbing stories of slavery and gender violence set against the backdrop of gleeful revelry. Approaching the front gate of the property, flanked as it was by a colorful display of Halloween hoopla—a large banner, white cutout ghosts, and huge freestanding letters that spelled out the word "Boo!"—did not alleviate the tension I felt.

At 7:45 P.M., I made my way from Live Oak Cabin, heading across the darkened grounds to take the evening Mystery Tour. A soft mist hung in the air, promising rain. I passed a pond surrounded by brush and a white wood palisade with a bridge arching over the shadowy water. Eager to reach the reassurance of bright lights that illuminated the Carriage House Restaurant, I hurried along the gravel path. Disembodied young voices were screaming with glee beyond the big house. Someone outside was sing-songing "They're h-e-r-e," the spooky line from Stephen Spielberg's film *Poltergeist*. I passed the Caretaker's Cottage, one of the haunted outbuildings on the plantation that was a favorite of tour groups. Five women lounged on the cottage's patio dressed in nightgowns and terrycloth robes, their hair wrapped in bath towels. "Don't let the ghosts get ya!" one of them called out to me as I walked by.

It was a strange night at The Myrtles, electric with the overnight guests' nervous energy and elevated expectations. The courtyard bustled with activity: visitors rocked in chairs on the back veranda, purchased drinks at the outdoor bar, shopped in the General's Store, and chased one another beneath the oaks. The crowd was mostly white and young to middle-aged. Besides me, there were just three other discernibly African American guests: a man and woman with their teenaged son. There were four children present in all. People waiting for the tour to begin were chatting with one another amiably. One woman in a bulky sweatshirt and baseball cap struck up a conversation with me. She said she had driven three and a half hours from Mississippi to tour The Myrtles. When I slipped into the General's Store only to return a few moments later, the woman in the sweatshirt said she had been looking for me to make sure I was a real person rather than a ghost. Out on the long L-shaped porch, strangers asked each other if they had "seen anybody yet" (meaning spirits) and conversed easily about topics that might have been avoided in meetings with strangers under regular circumstances: religious faith, spirituality, and belief in the supernatural. A self-professed atheist talked with a self-described Catholic about whether or not they believed in "this stuff." The Catholic woman started reciting her religious creed, demonstrating to the atheist how she would prepare herself for the tour. Another woman said she had been to several places on the most-haunted houses lists and never felt anything; still, here she was. A white lesbian couple talked with a Latino-white straight couple about the question of evidence and the power of suggestion. The man said he works in the field of mechanics and needs hard evidence in order to believe a claim. That's why he likes the show *Ghost Hunters*, he explained, because they go in trying to debunk specious accounts of hauntings. He was at The Myrtles for his wife. She had wanted to come here for a long time, so he had brought her for their "lucky 13th anniversary." His wife's dad, he added, was a ghost hunter. One of the women in the other couple said she was a scientist and always looks for rational explanations. She asked if anyone else had been on ghost tours in Savannah or New Orleans. "You have to go," she said. "There's so much history."

The guests who were gathered for The Myrtles Mystery Tour were from various segments of society—from the working class to the creative class to white-collar professionals. They were also from different parts of the country (including Wisconsin, Washington State, and California), though they skewed southern. They were thoughtful and interesting people with a range of interests in history, politics, and religious belief. They held divergent views about the afterlife and were willing to share those views with one another despite the generalized American sensitivity toward discussing religion in casual interactions. Visiting a "haunted" historic site drew them all together, dissolving barriers that normally separate people. The feeling of being at a special place with equally adventurous fellow sojourners charged up the crowd. The desire for interpersonal connection, as much as the prospect of encountering a ghost on the weekend before All Hallows' Eve, infused The Myrtles guests with convivial camaraderie. I found myself softening toward them as they absorbed me into their circle, questioning the sharp critique of The Myrtles that had been forming in my mind. And then our tour guide for the evening waved his hands over his head and clapped to claim our attention.

Our tour guide, whom I'll call Tommy, was a young African American man who spoke in southern-accented Black English when he warned the group not to "smudge up" the furniture. He sported long dreadlocks swinging from a slightly recessed hairline, lending him the self-styled look of a Maasai warrior. He wore a soft aqua top with dark blue sweatpants on his slender frame. Inside the house, Tommy began by telling us that he would be "starting with some history," but "it wouldn't be boring" because he would "give it oomph." In a blunt and cheeky speaking style, he recounted the story of David Bradford's role in the eighteenth-century Whiskey Rebellion, during which Bradford, founder of The Myrtles Plantation, is said to have bravely jumped from a building to escape President George Washington's militia. "Now we know it didn't happen like that," Tommy said, contradicting the common lore. "No man would be crazy enough to jump out of a high window." Right away, this tour guide had put our group on notice that he would be telling Myrtles tales even while he undercut them. "We have the stories," Tommy said, "but we know there is something else, something different, or something more to it."

He climbed the main staircase halfway so that he was poised above us as if on a stage, and from there he launched into the signature Myrtles Plantation story. With an animated face and gesticulating arms, he told us about how Judge Woodruff strode into his cotton fields over a hundred years ago, took a liking to a slave, brought her home, and made her his mistress. "Her name was," Tommy said and then waited, gesturing to the group with his hands for an answer. "Chloe!" the group recited in unison. Tommy nodded, picking up the reigns of his narrative and telling the group that Chloe soon began listening in on the judge's business meetings. When the judge caught her eavesdropping at the door of the men's parlor one day, he cut her ear off and demoted her to a kitchen slave. She started wearing a green turban to hide her ear and sought to get back into the family's good graces. She made a birthday cake with a little oleander poison, so that the two Woodruff girls would get sick and she would have to be called upon to nurse them back to health. Her plan went awry, however, when the mother and one of the daughters died. The judge was not there to eat the cake because he was, Tommy said with a knowing inflection, "taking care of some business out in the cotton fields." In response to his sexual innuendo, the other black woman in the group responded "Mmm Hmm," a sarcastic cultural vernacular rife with moral judgment. A white woman chimed in: "Chloe should have slapped the hell out of that judge." Tommy left space for these responses and then picked up his story line. Chloe, he told us, felt bad about the cake and confessed. As a result, a white and black mob hanged her to death by the riverside, weighing down her body with rocks. Because of her ugly death, Chloe haunts the place today. "You'll see her shadow or feel a chill on your arm or shoulder," Tommy told us. "Just let her pass. She'll do no harm."

"By the way," Tommy teased the group at the end of his story, "if y'all have seen that Discovery Channel or Travel Channel show on the place showing Chloe, that ain't no woman actress, that's me. Look at the face, y'all," he said, sweeping his long hair back. "Look at the face." Tommy held his pose for a moment like a contestant in a 1980s black gay Voguing contest and then directed our attention to the haunted mirror. He stepped lightly down the staircase, casually mentioning that since his grandmother was a Voodoo priestess, he knew all about the southern practice of covering mirrors after someone died. But when a member of our group asked him about Voodoo in response, he demurred, saying, "You don't want to go into all that. Trust me." He told us that people speculated about the discoloration in the mirror being the trapped spirits of Sarah Woodruff and her kids. His take, though, was that the streaks represented the Mississippi River and Chloe's watery demise.

In the women's parlor Tommy admonished a guest staying overnight who asked if she could "string up" a haunted doll in her bedroom in the house. He reacted with staged shock and said, "If you want to mess with the spirits, honey, that's on you. Do it after I've gone home." He turned his attention to the whole group then and told us, "Don't go looking for ghosts. People who look for spirits don't find them. Those who experience them tend to not be looking, like children, or nonbelievers who write strange sensations off as just being the air conditioning fan." In the dining room Tommy told a story about the visit of two blonde-haired New York City reporters who were "supposedly famous." They returned to their room in The Myrtles to find their clothes tossed about and a chair turned upside down. "I thought they were arrogant," he said. "Maybe the ghosts thought so too."

Tommy's final story was about Cleo. He showed us a portrait on the sitting-room wall of a girl in a tartan dress and said this was the child who had died from yellow fever back in the 1800s. A Voodoo priestess was brought in from Solitude Plantation to nurse the girl, he told us. She placed a gris-gris bag under the floorboards and said the girl would be better the next day, but instead of recovering, the girl died. The Stirling family, owners of the Myrtles at that time, hanged Cleo in the bedroom above the back parlor and sunk her lifeless body in the river. Tommy told us then that he is descended from slaves from The Myrtles and another nearby plantation and that plantations "used to litter this place." At end of the tour Tommy invited us to look at the photo of Chloe up close, walk around the plantation grounds, or "just sit and think." The suggestion that we turn our minds to deliberate contemplation was the last thing Tommy said to our tour group.

I stayed behind and asked Tommy if he wouldn't mind answering a question: he had said he was descended from slaves around here, so what did it mean to him to be telling these stories about Chloe and Cleo? He answered, "It makes me feel that generations have passed. That times have changed. I'm a descendant who can tell their story. And we can all hear it together, no matter our sexuality, race, or religion. That's what it means to me." A man who had hung back after the tour as well overheard Tommy's comment and joined our conversation. "How do the spirits feel about gays?" he asked, and then he explained that he was there with his male partner and twin kids, and with his sister, who was lesbian. (She was, it turned out, the woman who said Chloe should have slapped the judge.) Tommy threw his hands onto his hips: "The spirits better not care, because *I'm* gay." The two men talked then, exchanging stories about prejudice against gay men and women and prejudice against blacks. The visitor said it must be hard for Tommy, being in the South, but Tommy rejected that interpretation, saying no one ever bothers him; this was his home, and he and his friends "made damn sure that everybody knows that wouldn't be acceptable."

I left the two men talking together and went outdoors to gather my thoughts. In his unique version of the Mystery Tour, Tommy had accomplished an indirect yet effective critique of the dark-tourism plantation experience. Through irony, humor, and intelligent play, he destabilized the standard narrative of The Myrtles hauntings. He had opened his tour by telling us to question the stories and concluded it by telling us to think. He shifted minor details of the stories to portray nuanced emotion on the part of black characters, such as Chloe's remorse about the oleander cake. He enacted what black queer theorist E. Patrick Johnson has called a "quare vernacular performance," using the staircase of an old plantation house as his stage.[44] On that stage, Tommy initiated a call-and-response exchange, encouraging outspoken feedback on Chloe's history. He also performed virtual drag, using his fingers to frame a face that we were to imagine as feminized, flipping his dreadlocks over his shoulder, and sweeping his hands down the length of his body to indicate a dress, to become, briefly, a woman before us. Finally, he claimed knowledge and authority through the stereotyped trope of the Voodoo priestess yet refused to feed visitors' voyeuristic interest in the subject.

Tommy's emphasis on his role as storyteller in response to my question struck me as especially evocative. As a slave woman whose right to listen was violently policed, Chloe had been subject to her master's speech, to his structuring of reality. But in Tommy's version of the Mystery Tour, he was the speaker instead of the slaveholding judge. What is more, Tommy informed us that he often plays Chloe on television travel shows, that he had, in a sense, a dual persona as a black man in the present and a slave woman in the past. Through his dramatization as Chloe and revelation of that role, he was performing a doubling move to become Chloe's virtual doppelganger. With his voice, then, Tommy could project Chloe's voice. Chloe was the speaker now, and we paying tourists were the ones listening in. Tommy achieved, through strategic disclosure and "transgressive performance," a subtle symbolic reversal of plantation power dynamics.[45]

Tommy's black queer Mystery Tour had its limitations, both ideologically and effectively. He still recounted stories of violence against black women with a cheekiness that conveyed humor. He was still part of the dark-tourism commercial enterprise that objectified, erotized, and exoticized the suffering of enslaved black women in sensationalized scenes of subjection. He was a black man of the twenty-first century and not a black woman of the nineteenth century and could not claim to really know her subject position. But on that night during Tommy's tour I saw for the first time what I would describe as a usable take on plantation ghost tourism. Tommy teased and rebuked his mostly white, mostly southern audience, disabusing them of any sense that these romantic plantation stories were complete or fully authentic. He returned dignity to the figure of the black slave woman by inviting criticism of her treatment and by naming himself as a descendant in a way that grounded the stories he told in a context of human ties. He implied that plantation culture was little more than trash by saying that plantations had once "littered" the area. He articulated the value of people from various identity affiliations learning how to listen together and, more, learning how to listen to marginalized voices in our society, such as the voice of a young black southern gay man and an enslaved black girl. Tommy's style of communication was pleasing enough that he garnered praise and plentiful tips. When I commented to the Myrtles manager on how engaging the tour had been that night, she replied, "Everybody loves Tommy. People request him. He's a free spirit. You can't tie him down." Tourists were apparently willing, even eager, to hear a spirited perspective from an unlikely source even though it challenged conventional expectations.

Spending time at The Myrtles on Halloween left me with the feeling that it might just be possible to position "haunted" plantation sites in a manner that is politically conscious *and* attractive to visitors. But accomplishing this end would take site owners and community stakeholders who value public education over profit enough to produce informative written and digital materials about the lives of slaves. It would take site managers with a commitment to employing and rewarding creative tour guides from diverse backgrounds. It would take a concerted effort on the part of guides as well as tourists to integrate critical analyses of the past. And it would take the courage of us all not to hide from history's ghosts.

A Revisitation of Spirits

You must always choose the integrity of your ancestors.
—Tracey Hucks, *Yoruba Traditions and African American
Religious Nationalism* (2012)

*Cheese Grits and Slave Ghosts:
Market Notes from a Dark-Tourism Journey*

I am haunted by homes from the past and the people who occupied them. This is why I write history, I think, dwelling on what once was and peering into domestic realms where intimate human dramas unfold, scene by scene and century by century. A fascination with dead people and old places is what led me to Savannah on a dreary long weekend in February 2012. My goal was to take in the city's antique atmosphere while observing the portrayals of slaveholders and the enslaved in manor homes of the famed historic district. But I got far more than I bargained for in one of Savannah's charming squares. As a tour guide in New Orleans would later warn was possible, a ghost had attached herself and followed me home. This ghost, an enslaved girl named Molly, led me on a journey of discovery, contemplation, and confrontation with my own beliefs and with the phenomenon of dark tourism.

After encountering Molly in the form of her ghost story, I set out to broaden my firsthand experience with haunted historic sites of the South. I wanted to see these places up close, to learn what stories were told about them, by whom, to whom, and toward what ends. My hunt for slave ghosts propelled by that first visit to the Sorrel-Weed House began with a return to Savannah and the broader coastal low-country region of Georgia and South Carolina, then moved inward to the Mississippi Valley of Louisiana. Along the way and over two years I traced what I see now as a trend in haunted slavery stories at historic sites.

Even the venerable Colonial Williamsburg institution in Virginia now advertises "a haunted history to tell" in the form of "family-friendly Ghost Walks" and a "Ghosts Among Us" evening tour.[1] Ghost tours tied to homes, cemeteries, inns, pubs, and other sites are crowding into the southern heritage and history market as the broader tourism industry feeds and foments a mass-culture interest in hauntings.

Tourism, the commercial environment in which ghost tours arose, has seen stupendous growth since 1990 and, according to journalist Elizabeth Becker, now employs one of every ten people on the globe. Becker calls tourism the "stealth industry of the twenty-first century," a massive sector of the world economy that is often overlooked in discussions of powerful industries such as oil, finance, and agriculture. As the tourism industry skyrocketed, it needed to diversify, to find new outlets and attract fresh markets. The practice that has come to be known as dark tourism is an outgrowth of this diversification, a "lucrative niche market," in Becker's words, which dominates particular historical sites. She offers as an example how tourists flock to the Tuol Sleng museum in Cambodia where the Khmer Rouge regime carried out torture and executions. Visitors are drawn by the opportunity to hear what Becker calls a story of "sadism and pain" and to witness the "cells and instruments of torture."[2] This interest seems to contradict the traditional idea of tourism as a practice characterized by pleasure and escape. But it is, in fact, the essence of dark tourism to bring together pleasure and pain, death and discovery, in touristic opportunities that highlight mortality, violence, atrocity, and suffering.

John Lennon and Malcolm Foley, professors of tourism in the United Kingdom, coined the term "dark tourism" in their coauthored book titled *Dark Tourism: The Attraction of Death and Disaster*. After conducting fieldwork across the world on the state of tourism in the 1990s, they observed, "It is clear from a number of sources that tourist interest in recent death, disaster and atrocity is a growing phenomenon in the late twentieth and early twenty-first centuries." Touristic travel to battlefields, cemeteries, and museums that commemorated atrocities such as the Jewish Holocaust was part of this trend. Lennon and Foley argued that the assemblage of "associated tourism products" that they were labeling "dark tourism" tapped into a fascination with death that sprang from anxieties about postmodern life: the condition of our present era that is characterized by cultural decentralization, spatial disorientation, and disassociation from traditional institutions. Dark tourism, Lennon and Foley explained, is an indirect means for the expression of public doubt about a shared subjectivity arising from key features of modernity, such as late capitalism, rational inquiry, and technological innovation.[3]

Scholars widely share this notion that the rise of dark tourism is tied to a broadly experienced contemporary worry about societal change at the start of the twenty-first century. "Millennial anxiety," the academic term for this feeling of unease, is also credited for the surge in popular interest in ghosts and the supernatural around the year 2000. Other causes that tourism theorists offer for the recent rise of dark tourism include "morbid curiosity," "a collective sense of identity and survival," "restorative nostalgia," "fear of phantoms," "search for novelty," "desire to celebrate crime or deviance," "basic bloodlust," and "dicing with death."[4] Growing anxiety about the signs and effects of climate change, financial collapse, and in the United States, both the decline of American global power and a decrease in traditional religious beliefs might also contribute to a cultural preoccupation with doom, death, and the afterlife. And surely the human preoccupation with death spans time periods. As the only species that knows we will one day die, people are burdened with questions of what life should mean for us, how death will come, and what, if anything, occurs on the other side of that mysterious divide.

As more and more people demonstrate their interest in visiting disturbing sites, the number of entrepreneurs willing to provide dark-tourism experiences steadily increases. Richard Sharpley, a tourism professor in the United Kingdom, explains in his coedited book, *The Darker Side of Travel: The Theory and Practice of Dark Tourism*, that "over the last half century and commensurate with the remarkable growth in general tourism, dark tourism has become more widespread and diverse. . . . There appears to be an increasing number of people keen to promote and or profit from 'dark' events as tourist attractions."[5] A lucrative segment of the tourism industry now specializes in the commodification of death, and mainstream tourism outlets are quickly incorporating paranormal experiences into their grab bag of offerings. Ghost tourism, which is steadily competing with traditional tourism in America's historic places, is one of dark tourism's most seductive forms precisely because it projects feelings of fun and frivolity onto histories of trauma.

The U.S. South, with its history of Indian removal, slavery, and bloody Civil War battles, together with its regional particularity and atmospheric setting of simmering heat and shroud-like Spanish moss, is a place easily associated with a dark past and a haunted present. In the South, the term "dark tourism" thus takes on a second, racialized dimension, as the practice of this pursuit in the region often incorporates slavery and the African American experience. The merger of dual primal fears—the human fear of death and the southern (indeed, American) fear of blackness—makes dark tourism in the South all the more potent. The southern ghost tour, in the form of both exterior walking tours and interior historic home tours, has therefore become a regular feature of the touristic landscape, building on the traditional literary form of the southern gothic novel, the popularity of heritage tourism in the 1980s–90s, and the contemporary cultural trend of ghost fancy. In the wake of my travels, I find it a matter of serious concern that ghost tourism has gained a firm foothold within the boundaries of the former Old South, where the bodies of black slaves have once again become fodder for an innovating capitalist industry. Historian Edward Baptist has shown that in the antebellum era, the new formula for creating southern wealth was black bodies producing bales of cotton on former American Indian lands. The growth of dark tourism strongly suggests that a current formula for commercial success is black ghosts producing spectacles of slavery at storied historic sites.[6] Although these spectacles are taking place below the Mason-Dixon line, now, as in the early to mid-1800s, regional lines are false indicators of the wide reach of this commercial enterprise. The profits of slavery enmeshed the North as well as the South, leading to, as historian Joshua Rothman has put it, "imbrications of supposedly free financial markets with the foul violence of slavery."[7] Today visitors from around the country, and indeed, the world, participate in these spectacles of slavery as global tourism expands. And in the age of digital technology and media, the reach of southern spectral imagery stretches farther than ever before, casting a shadow beyond regional and even national space to make the enslaved black body of the American past ever more profitable.

That Old Black Magic: Ghost Tours, Voodoo, and Slave Religion

If the ghost and cemetery tours that I took in Savannah, New Orleans, and Charleston had one element in common, it would be the appropriation of black slave religion. Voodoo was the spiritual practice of choice on these tours; the belief in spirits held by Gullah and Geechee people came in at a close second. Tour scripts highlighted black spiritual and folk beliefs passed down from enslaved ancestors as exotic tidbits that enhanced haunted story lines. Guides referenced Voodoo and haints to infuse paranormal claims with geographical particularity and to increase the level of threat and titillation that comes with the southern dark-tourism package. The specialness and danger that tour companies sought to incorporate through references to Voodoo and haints were racialized elements, made more strange, exciting, and threatening because of the blackness of the spiritual adherents. Viewed in mainstream American cultural belief as a black African religion, Voodoo represents the ultimate opposite to Western Christian faith. Voodoo is assumed to be pagan, demonic, erotic, naturalistic, animalistic, and subversive. In its perceived alterity and negativity, Voodoo is inaccessible to Western thought. The lack of understanding of the moral principles upon which Voodoo operates as a belief system feeds many Americans' sense of fear and anxiety about the faith. In the face of Voodoo and other African-based spiritualities, mainstream Americans often feel mystified and out of control. While confusion and abandon may be undesirable emotions in everyday, conscious life, they become desirable emotions in the ghost-tour framework in which cultural taboos are expected to be broken. As the "savage" religion of racialized slaves, the ultimate subjugated group in U.S. history, Voodoo becomes the symbol for a dark spiritual plane, for secret lives, and for the subversive impulse. The slave ghost who returns from the dead to haunt the subconscious of American national identity must bring Voodoo ritual along to seal the deal.

The less-formalized Gullah and Geechee spiritual beliefs serve the same purpose in the places where they are locally expressed, the Georgia and South Carolina coasts. For who better than African slaves practicing a pagan faith would represent vengeful spirits, death, and the utter depths of the dark side? Participants in ghost tours are invited to play with these elements, to project themselves, for the time of the tour, into the dark realm of the "other"—the ultimate opposite, the African slave. As author Toni Morrison has theorized in her study of the black figure in the American literary canon, "The dramatic polarity created by skin color, the projection of the not-me" resulted in a "playground for the imagination" of white Americans.[8]

The gris-gris bag I was given in New Orleans, the stories of root work I listened to in Savannah, and the tales of haint blue I heard in Charleston were plucked and packaged for popular consumption. These mentions barely skimmed the surface of slave religion and missed its import for the black experience as well as the human experience. While ghost and cemetery tours picked and chose selective bits from black religious beliefs in order to localize and dramatize their paranormal narratives, scholarship on slave religion has thoughtfully explained the variety, richness, and liberating purpose of African American faith during slavery. In his classic study *Slave Religion*, historian Albert Raboteau called black spirituality the "invisible institution" of the antebellum era. He argued that African American faith as practiced in the South was a syncretic belief system formed from the slaves' African past combined with their experience in new American environments. Enslaved blacks adapted their fundamental belief in the power of spirits in the world to novel and trying circumstances. Practiced in the secret spaces of the slave quarters or woods, African American religion included a series of key elements: belief in a high god and sometimes lesser divinities; perception of a rich and active spirit world in which the ancestors participate; respect for elders; serious attention to burial rites; expressive practices of dancing, drumming, and singing as forms of worship; and an incorporation of nature in practice and ritual. As enslaved blacks encountered Christian beliefs in the American states and began to convert in larger numbers in the late 1700s and early 1800s, they redirected many of these features of worship toward a Christian God.[9]

While part of black religious life in the South, Voodoo was a particular kind of spiritual expression that changed over time. Raboteau explains that Voodoo first began as an organized belief system sustained by scrupulous adherents. Brought to the United States by Haitian and other French Caribbean slaves, Voodoo had developed from African roots. The faith swelled in New Orleans and greater Louisiana in the aftermath of the Haitian Revolution as large numbers of black Haitians immigrated to the region. Men and, more often, women functioned as priests and priestesses of the faith. In the late nineteenth century, what had been a holistic belief system dissipated into a set of disparate practices. Practitioners sustained "root work" (the use of roots and natural objects for the purposes of protection and harming) as part of their spiritual tradition and distributed magical charms or "gris-gris" to believers. The magical aspect of Voodoo mirrored belief in the power of spirits and charmed objects, especially natural objects, found in other expressions of slave religion. Over time, Voodoo rituals and similar magical practices expressed by slaves outside New Orleans and without Caribbean backgrounds came to be associated.

Black slaves as well as observers beyond slave communities used the same terms—"voodoo," "hoodoo," and "root work"—to refer to acts of conjuring that once had been associated with distinct strands of slave religion. Religious historian Yvonne Chireau defines the particularities and overlap of these terms, detailing that "Hoodoo" referred to spells of "magical manipulation" but could also refer to "healing and harming traditions"; that "root work" referred to the use of natural objects in ritual; and that "Voodoo" (or "Vodou") referred to a religion that blacks brought from Haiti in the late 1700s and early 1800s. However, African Americans often used the term "Voodoo" synonymously with "Hoodoo" and "tricking," meaning the use of "spiritual powers for malevolent purposes."[10]

These varied African diasporic spiritual practices designated by interchangeable terms have in common a foundational connection to the Yoruba religion based in Nigeria. Slaves transported and transformed elements of Yoruba (as well as other West and Central African beliefs) when they were forcibly relocated to the Caribbean, Latin America, and North America through the crucible of the transatlantic slave trade. Religion scholar Tracey Hucks argues in her study of Yoruba traditions in America that it was important to the enslaved to call forth the "image and symbol of Africa as a religious orientation" in order to create a sense of home in America. "Yoruba religion," she writes, "invokes a meaningful connection to Africa as 'originary space' that substantiates human value and provides restorative ontological, historical, and spiritual integrity."[11] In the cauldron of chattel slavery, belief in a rich and potent African-inspired spirit world sustained black identity, strength, and will. Slave religion was a creative, heartfelt, and serious expression of slave life, of slaves as human beings *worthy* of dignified life and invested with spiritual efficacy. Southern blacks used their faith to establish who they were within, who they were in relation to one another, and who they were in relation to their condition of enslavement. They also used their faith to protect themselves—spiritually, psychologically and physically—from those who owned and oppressed them. Yvonne Chireau describes black slaves' "supernatural harming" traditions—favorite fodder for Voodoo fascination and revulsion in American culture—as a "force for self defense" within the context of slavery.[12] Working roots, creating charms, fashioning plant poisons, or calling on the spirits to prevent the sale of a loved one or ward off a beating gave enslaved blacks a critical sense of empowerment. Slave conjurers comforted and consoled their community members, people at perpetual risk.[13] Slave religion was therefore a "lifeline" for enslaved blacks, a "weapon for the weak."[14] This essential import of black religious practices as "cultural and spiritual resources" for the oppressed is lost in the ghost-tour industry.[15] When tour companies and tour guides strip out the emotional and historical significance of black spirituality in order to dangle tantalizing bits of racialized otherness and spiritual danger, they are exoticizing and commercializing historic sites and stories of the slaveholding South.

It is difficult to imagine that ghost tours would treat elements of the Christian faith, associated with whiteness and Western culture, in this disparaging way. Even Catholicism, which I sometimes saw invoked to lend mystery to southern cultures on the tourism circuit, is spared from being reduced to a dangerous (demonic) or superstitious (naive) belief system. Whether consciously or unconsciously, the ghost-tour guides I saw at work positioned black slave religion as less important, less serious, and less worthy of respect than Christian traditions. Even Karen Jeffries, a New Orleans tour guide whose gentle personality I appreciated, acted out this cultural hierarchy of race and religion in spatial terms. When discussing the history of white Catholic New Orleans, she sat our tour group down on the courthouse steps. But when telling the history of the slave trade and Voodoo faith, she had us stand outside a commercial Voodoo shop. The implicit contrast was striking. Black cultural history was not only positioned as less lofty than Euro-American cultural history in this unconscious spatial orientation, but it was also presented as a commodity. It is perhaps not surprising that this was the moment when members of the tour group began to inquire about where they could purchase authentic Voodoo dolls.

I cannot help but feel, after my experiences, that ghost tourism at southern sites borrows from African American cultural expression, especially religious expression, while simultaneously undermining the value of black history. And this dialectical incorporation and marginalization of black cultural elements on ghost tours, this pull in two opposing directions, resonates with how ghost stories function culturally. Just as ghost stories call to mind social memories that have been repressed, thereby revealing and yet also controlling disturbing knowledge about the past, ghost tours feature, but at the same time cloak, African American lives.

The Ghosts of Slavery: Recuperation at a Cost

It would be disingenuous of me not to acknowledge that ghost-tour companies are doing the work of making black history visible in some of this country's oldest places. In contrast to a growing number of haunted tours that actively incorporate African American stories, many plantation heritage tours continue to marginalize black personalities and historical experiences.[16] During my time in Savannah, I saw evidence of urban historian Ella Howard's observation that "the subset of paranormal tours pay much more attention to slavery than others."[17] In Charleston, the dearth of black history on offer by established companies was so great that tour guide Geordie Buxton suggested that I, an Ohioan with no special knowledge of Charleston history, should create my own black history tour in the city. Meanwhile, Buxton was interweaving snippets of black folklore and history into his haunted plantations tour. Ghost tours clearly represent a kind of cultural inclusion, but I have to press the question: At what cost? Much of the black history material that I encountered during my ghost-touring journey appeared to me as exoticized, romanticized, or decontextualized. And members of black communities did not seem to control the narratives of these tours or to benefit directly from the commercial success of local ghost-tour outfits.

I came away from my travels with an overwhelming feeling that ghost tourism at historic sites of slavery appropriates African American history in a way that outweighs the value of inclusion. Whether or not they are aware of it or want to be doing it, tourism professionals use black cultural knowledge (stories, beliefs, practices, and histories) to infuse southern ghost tours with a superficial sense of soul. The recuperated black slave in the form of a ghost is presented in caricature on these tours, positioned outside black cultural contexts, and stripped of the historical realities of American slavery. Experiences of black slaves and elements of black culture are thus diminished in this industry—borrowed, boiled down to an exotic essence, and sold for a price. Rather than finding an opportunity to learn about the antebellum past, to empathize with enslaved human beings, or to connect with a rich though troubled regional and national heritage, tourists encounter narratives that temper the history of slavery and race relations, assuage guilt, and feed fascination with the racialized other. The use of slaves' lives, likenesses, and experiences for the grist of this economic enterprise seems to amount to a virtual recommodification and recommercialization of black bodies in the modern moment. (As historian Farina Mir put it when I talked through my analysis with her and historian Paulina Alberto in attempt to pin down what I thought: "The other side of historical marginalization is turning out to be commodification, commercialization. And it is not unconscious.")

I also came away with an alarming sense that the representation of slaves as ghosts reproduces intersectional racial and gender norms from the antebellum era, often without context, caution, or critique. As a result, the narratives on these tours reinforce retrograde interpretations of power, race, gender, sexuality, and identity. These stories turn on the abuse of the socially weak, often African American women, but do nothing to contextualize the experiences of black women or hold accountable the perpetrators of violence against them. In short, ghost tours featuring spectral slaves often uphold the ideas of an antebellum social order by replaying antebellum plots that repopularize antiquated race and gender hierarchies. The reproduction of these plots is intensified by the use of digital technology that makes possible the easy duplication and dissemination of black women's suffering. Ghost tours and their widely circulated stories featuring enslaved black ghosts do the important cultural work of raising the subject of slavery but ultimately romanticize and reinforce unjust social relations from a bygone era.

Though mostly absent on the tours that I took, Native Americans are also part of this picture of a haunted southern past. I encountered four mentions of indigenous people during my travels. On the Ghost Walk of Saint Simons (billed as the original ghost tour on the Georgia island) the colorful guide was an actor who told our group he had appeared in several History Channel productions. He played his part to the hilt in period dress as he led us by lantern light through a parklike area that he said had once been an Indian burial ground. In the Haunted History of New Orleans tour, the guide proclaimed that cannibal Indians had performed their sacred rituals in the spot where the city's deadly fires had later erupted. In books about The Myrtles Plantation in Louisiana, authors credit the plantation with being built (or not being built—this is a matter of contention) on ancient Tunica burial grounds.[18] The fourth reference to native people occurred on an African American heritage tour to which I will return. These references to American Indians, which were all quite brief, highlighted long-standing stereotypes of native savagery and native disappearance. The main point encapsulated in these mentions was that native people were present only as part of the land-scape, existing before history rather than within it and creating the sur-face upon which the dramas of other groups would later play out.

I found the state of the southern ghost tour as I observed it over two years of travel to be dark indeed. But the ghost-tour industry in the South has likely grown even larger in the time that it took me to write this book. Along the way, I became obsessed by my hunt for Molly, fas-cinated by my fellow tourists, enthralled by veteran storytellers, and moved by the histories of southern lands. I have to ask myself now, as I asked geographer Glenn Gentry at the start of my research: Why? Why ghosts? My answer: Because ghosts represent history in a way that feels like magic. The magic of the ghost story is an intensified version of the magic of historical interpretation writ large—the weaving of words, ideas, and events into a pseudo-spell that can spirit us back to days gone by. The desire for historical intimacy that many of us have can be satisfied through visits to "haunted" places, which allow people to touch the past in both material and immaterial ways. There is a lasting allure in hauntings. American culture, southern culture, will not give up the ghost. And if I am honest with myself and with you, neither have I.

When I spent the night at The Myrtles Plantation in St. Francisville, Louisiana, I had already heard the tale about Chloe the slave. Her mas-ter had cut off one of her ears in punishment for eavesdropping, and, as the story goes, Chloe's ghost floats across the Myrtles grounds today, stealing just one earring from female guests. During my first night on the plantation, I kept my earrings on. When I awoke, one silver hoop was missing. I felt a sudden shock of panic when I touched my bare ear and realized this. A few mad moments later, after I had searched between the sheets and on the floor, all the while telling myself that my mounting anxiety was ridiculous, I found the missing earring at the foot of the bed. Chloe had not taken it. But maybe some part of me had wanted to believe that she could, to believe that any African American woman who lived in the worst of times could communicate with me, a descendant of those lost generations. Part of me wanted Chloe to be real, to make herself known, to materialize. How different am I, really, from the thousands of tourists who seek out haunted history experi-ences? As conscientious thinkers who care about our individual and collective engagement with the past, I do not believe we can simply dis-miss the southern ghost tour as popular-culture fluff. But I do think we can imagine other ways, better ways, to conjure the ghosts of slavery.

Ghost in the Machine: Haunting and the
African American Storytelling Tradition

Black slaves do not fare well in the genre of the southern ghost tour. But we need not rely on ghost tours and haunted sites to gain historical understanding about the supernatural in African American experience. We have at our disposal a wealth of interpretive knowledge in the African American cultural tradition that takes up the subject of ghosts in stories dating back to the time of slavery. African American stories grounded in history can function as counterpoints to popular, for-profit ghost-tourism tales. Here too, ghosts represent the past and serve as a marker of historical memory, but they represent a past with teeth, a past that is rife with trauma and the terror that characterizes the experience of an oppressed people. In African American tales of haunting, spirits of the dead are neither frivolous nor romantic. Their presence signals a need for those in the present to deal directly with a dangerous past that will not rest.

Former slaves in Georgia interviewed by employees of the Federal Writers' Project in the 1930s sometimes recalled stories of ghosts and hauntings. When not directly elicited by the interviewer, their references to ghosts were rare, indicating that this was a subject the speakers preferred not to discuss. The stilted question posed by federal interviewers about ghosts during slavery treated the topic as child's play, fun and games, or fanciful superstition. Interviewers were prompted by project guidelines to ask as question number 13, "What games did you play as a child? Can you give the words or sing any of the play songs or ring game of the children? Riddles? Charms? Stories about 'Raw Head and Bloody Bones' or other 'hants' or ghosts? Stories about animals? What do you think of Voodoo? Can you give the words or sign any lullabies? Work songs? Plantation hollers? Can you tell a funny story you have heard or something funny that happened to you? Tell about the ghosts you have seen."[19] Despite this prompt that misunderstood, trivialized, and collapsed various black cultural practices, former slaves who responded to the question resisted the categorization of hauntings as mere childish fun. The stories they told about ghosts include a persistent theme: a view of spirits of the dead as powerful, potentially harmful entities to be both respected and feared. Carrie Nancy Fryer, for instance, said that she had been born with a caul, a thin layer of membrane over the head and face that has signified double sight into the spirit world in African American understandings. Because of the caul, Fryer was able to see ghosts from early childhood on, but she did not flaunt this ability. She heeded the words of her mother, who told her, "Now Nancy, you know you [can] see [them], but . . . [y]ou mus[t] keep it to yourself." Emmaline Kilpatrick told her interviewer that she and other people she knew feared ghosts as well as graveyards and carried rabbits' feet for protection. Frances Kimbrough reported seeing her former master appear as a ghost who still exercised his power of surveillance while "watchin[g] us free [blacks] w[o]rkin[g]."[20]

And the richest tale of haunting in the Georgia WPA slave narratives comes from Emmaline Heard, a woman whose terrifying story symbolically represented the deadly profit-centered grind of slavery. Heard recounted her mother's escape from the plantation after being whipped by her mistress. During a desperate, moonlit flight, Heard's mother had to pass by a haunted cemetery. The woman heard a loud, clanging sound of "wheels and chains," like a machine in motion. She saw "a big thing as large as a house" that "looked like a lot of chains, wheels posts all mangled together." Emmaline Heard recounted that the spot where her mother had seen that "machine" of a "thing" was still haunted at the time that Heard told this story to the WPA interviewer. The reason for the haunting, she said, "was because old Dave Copeland used to whip his slaves to death and bury them along there." In Emmaline Heard's astute story, slavery is a monstrous, industrial machine that consumed African American lives and continues to haunt the southern landscape even after emancipation.[21]

Stories told by African Americans who experienced slavery indicate their belief that ghosts were dangerously real and not to be dallied with. One particularly symbolic story from the WPA narratives suggested that the system of slavery itself could best be represented as a ghostly entity. Generations later, the notion of the threat posed by ghosts and the nightmare of being haunted by slavery appeared in an intuitive work of African American and American letters: Toni Morrison's classic novel *Beloved*. In *Beloved*, a slave child representing the history of slavery returns to haunt her mother in the Reconstruction-era North, capturing, and perhaps channeling, this culturally resonant concept of the fiendish, frightful ghost of slavery.[22]

Black Heritage and the Hearse: Moving beyond the Ghost Tour

The southern tourism market is dominated by mainstream companies and prevailing cultural narratives, but African American voices can and do push through the noise. The narratives told in black social circles and on black-owned historical tours emphasize the trials and triumphs of a proud heritage and duplicate the pattern evidenced in slave narratives and black contemporary fiction of respect for and wariness of spirits. Two cases in particular, one from New Orleans and the other from Savannah, demonstrate this perspective. In order to help with my project, Elizabeth James, an Afro-Native storyteller with family roots in New Orleans, convened an informal focus group of five African American men and women in 2014 to discuss the topic of the Lalaurie mansion, the "haunted house" on Royal Street. All of the group members were forty to sixty years old, hailed from the Tremé neighborhood, and had long been actively involved in black civic life in New Orleans. Over cafés au lait and beignets in City Park, they discussed Madame Lalaurie and her treatment of her bondspeople. They found that from the time they were children, they had each been warned by elders in the black community to avoid that "bad house." Elizabeth James dated her family's oral admonition about the Lalaurie mansion back to 1905, when her grandmother's grandmother passed down "bad feelings surrounding the house." Rather than seeking to investigate the haunted premises, commune with ghosts, or lead tours for profit, African Americans in New Orleans, at least in this discussion group, seem to have passed down a sense of foreboding about the Lalaurie place. The Lalaurie house fire, in the view of the men and women gathered in City Park, represented the "epitome of the horrors of slavery" in a time and place where "the cruelty of slavery was accepted." In contrast to members of the tourist industry (who, in every case that I observed, were Euro-American), these black city residents revealed an orientation of distance and caution in relationship to what they called the "dark house" with a "dark heart." In addition to avoiding Lalaurie's tainted home, uppermost on their minds was the call to show respect for the enslaved people who had lived and suffered there. Elizabeth James recounted that when passing the haunted house on Royal Street, she was instructed by her grandmother to "cross to the other side of the street and make the sign of the cross, both for protection and in honor of the ancestors."[23]

Respect for the ancestral dead and an avoidance of ghost-tour culture was also the predominant theme of the Freedom Trail Black History Tour in Savannah, owned and operated by Johnnie Brown. The Freedom Trail Tour did not take reservations and departed from the Visitor Center at 1:00 and 3:00 P.M. each day. The tour guide, an African American man in young middle age, delivered his historically detailed narrative to a group of six on the day that I climbed into his van. Four of those six were elderly whites; one was a black man from Atlanta who had come down expressly for this tour. The tour that let out before ours had four passengers, all African American women. Our guide was dressed in a designer ensemble of matching denim shirt and shorts with colorful quiltlike blocks of color. He wore a straw hat and alligator sandals. He spoke or, rather, lectured to those on the van in a thick southern accent bathed in serious tones that conveyed his clear intent that we leave his tour with an appreciation for black historical struggles in the city of Savannah.

Brown drove us all around the city to complete his wide-ranging itinerary, including to black neighborhoods west and east, where he pointed out a structure painted "haint blue" but did not dwell on the term or even explain its meaning. He took us to the riverfront where slaves were disgorged into early Savannah and had us walk into the cavernous, stone enclosure where he said slaves were first held after disembarking from ships. Brown related with detail the strategic location of colonial Georgia as a buffer to keep slaves from escaping from the Carolinas into Florida. He talked about the forced removal of Indian tribes in the state and stressed the Seminole alliance with escaped black slaves down in the Florida swamps. He talked about black fugitives escaping to Fort Mose in Florida rather than north to Canada. He took us to First Baptist and Second Baptist Church, emphasizing the pride of the mostly enslaved congregations in building their own houses of worship. He took us to the monument for black Haitian soldiers who fought in the American Revolution as allies of the states.

Finally, Brown took our group to Laurel Grove, a black cemetery on the edge of town that had been restored through the effort of W. W. Law, Brown's deceased mentor and a civil rights leader in the city. Brown repeated Law's name over and over again on the tour, fixing it into our memories. He wanted us to recognize and honor this black civic leader and his accomplishments; he wanted us to have respect for the dead. Unlike the centrally located Colonial Cemetery that appears on most ghost tours in Savannah, Laurel Grove was located on the grounds of a former plantation. Brown pointed out gnarled old trees—"whipping trees," he called them—showing us marks left on the bark presumably from the stripes of punishment meted out to slaves. He identified worn stone markers placed for slaves and then quietly stepped back, modeling a moment of silence that reflected an African American conscientiousness toward burial sites dating back to the era of slave religion. Brown said nothing about ghosts or hauntings and nothing about Voodoo, and he spun no cemetery lore based on Gullah or Geechee tradition. When I asked him if he had heard the stories about dead slaves told on the local ghost tours, he made a sound like a scoff and said, simply, no. His intention, his object, like that of his mentor before him, was to honor in death those communal ancestors who had been dishonored in life.

As we drove away from the cemetery, a memory trove for African American community members who had spent a generation restoring it, two small black cats crossed the street in front of the tour van. No one commented on bad luck or black magic. No one dared. My thoughts, and perhaps the thoughts of my companions, were fixed on the souls—former slaves—whose graves we had just visited. The spirit of Johnnie Brown's heritage tour was the antithesis of ghost tours that I had taken in Savannah. He emphasized personal strength, a quest for freedom, and pride of community. Everything about his tour—his tone, his posture, his demeanor, and his stories—stressed the dignity and perseverance of black life, a dignity that his tour of Savannah ably reflected.

After our tour, Brown pulled into his designated spot in the parking lot of the Savannah Visitor Center. A gray hearse used for the Hearse Ghost Tours company pulled up beside him; it was a company whose guides I had seen stopping in front of the Sorrel-Weed House to tell the sordid story of Molly the murdered slave girl. As I took in the picture of these two vehicles side by side—the silly ghost-tour hearse and the serious black heritage van—I was struck by the contrast. The black heritage tourism industry is not without its complications, its internal divisions and compromises with commercial markets and public constituencies. But black heritage tourism surely stands on higher ground than the brand of tourism represented by that hearse. There are alternatives to the soulless enterprise of selling slavery as mainstream ghost tourism. African American heritage tourism and public history scholarship, African American storytelling performances, historic site blogs, and literature—all seem good starting points for affirming black dignity of

Tour vehicles in the Savannah Visitor Center parking lot. This Ghost Hearse Tours vehicle and Freedom Trail Black History Tour van were parked side by side in the parking lot of the Visitor Center. Photo by the author, 2013.

the past while not denying the cultural power of death, haunting, and the spiritual realm.[24] For my small part, I was inspired to write a ghost into the center of my novel about the Cherokee plantation owned by James Vann, the secret project that I carried along on that first trip to Savannah. She is a mixed-race African American and Native American adolescent girl ghost whose personal calling is history. Seeing the past through this ghost's eyes means confronting the pain as well as the persistence of the enslaved and free women who mothered her. While I was working on the novel (and still keeping quiet about it), I asked my friend Julia Autry, interpretive ranger of the Chief Vann House Historic Site, what she thought about ghost tours. She told me, "It drives me nuts that the big push in house museums is about ghost tours. People constantly ask if the [Vann] house is haunted. They say they saw something in the cellar or heard something in the attic. People ask me to confirm the orbs in their photos. They don't remember the history. All they remember is ghosts."[25] Given what I have seen in the South, I cannot deny the clarity of her insight. But I hope that she will accept, and maybe even come to embrace, my attempt to imagine a ghost worth remembering at the plantation site that she cares for, a ghost whose sole purpose it is to call to mind the solemn past of that place.[26]

During my journey, I saw firsthand how African American slaves are figured into a booming ghost-tourism industry that plays on ideas of the past. But how would the people held as slaves represent their own experience if they could commune with us now? I do not have the power to channel voices of the dead claimed by some of the psychics described in these pages. But I do have—we all have—the resource of a wise and haunting African American cultural tradition. This tradition tells us, as storyteller Elizabeth James put it, that when it comes to ghosts in the black experience, "This isn't Casper." African American spirits are not gullibly friendly, delightfully cartoonish, or controllably mainstream. They are deadly serious messengers from another time that compel us to wrestle with the past, a past chained to colonialism, slavery, and patriarchy, but a past that can nevertheless challenge and commission us to fight for justice in the present. We *can* call forth the power of ghosts as scholars, writers, artists, teachers, and stewards of historic sites, as indeed we must if we are to place progressive social justice visions in contention with a culture possessed by ghost fancy. But let our ghosts be real, let our ghosts be true, let our ghosts carry on the integrity of our ancestors.[27]

Notes

PREFACE

1. Anne Mitchell Whisnant, Marla R. Miller, Gary B. Nash, and David Thelen, *Imperiled Promise: The State of History in the National Park Service*, completed by the Organization of American Historians at the invitation of the National Park Service (Bloomington, Ind.: Organization of American Historians, 2011), 6.

2. For more on the Owens-Thomas House, see Tania June Sammons, *The Owens-Thomas House* (Savannah: Telfair Books, 2009). For more on the Telfairs as slaveholders, see "'To Venerate the Spot' of 'Airy Visions': Slavery and the Romantic Conception of Place in Mary Telfair's Savannah," in *Slavery and Freedom in Savannah*, ed. Leslie M. Harris and Daina Ramey Berry (Athens: University of Georgia Press, 2014), 69–92.

3. Paul C. Bland, *The Savannah Guidebook: The Essential Guide to Historic Savannah* (Savannah: Coastal Books & Souvenirs, 2010). See also Georgia Historic Places, Savannah Historic District, National Park Service, U.S. Department of the Interior, http://www.nps.gov/nr/travel/geo-flor/1.htm (accessed January 18, 2013).

4. The characteristics ascribed to Sorrel's Caribbean heritage in the tour narrative (bright colors and superstition) should not be read as culturally revealing. These elements, like others of the tour, mixed audience expectation and stereotype in ways that are not reliably informative of the family's actual beliefs.

INTRODUCTION

1. Ikam Acosta, "Seven Best Ghost and Paranormal Shows," *Huffington Post*, September 1, 2010, www.aoltv.com/2010/09/01/seven-best-ghost-and-paranormal-shows/ (accessed September 25, 2013).

2. Elizabeth Becker, *Overbooked: The Exploding Business of Travel and Tourism* (New York: Simon and Schuster, 2013), 16, 17.

3. Margaret Wayt DeBolt, *Savanah Spectres and Other Strange Tales* (1984; reprint, Norfolk, Va.: Donning Co., 2010); Robert Edgerly, *Savannah Hauntings: A Walking Tourist Guidebook* (Savannah: See Savannah Books, 2005); Nancy Roberts, *Georgia Ghosts* (1997; reprint, Winston-Salem, N.C.: John F. Blair, 2008).

4. A special issue of the *South Carolina Review* features the work of several scholars present at that SASA conference. See Sarah Juliet Lauro and Kimberly Manganelli, eds., *South Carolina Review* 47, no. 2, Spectral South special issue (Spring 2015).

5. Geordie Buxton, *Haunted Plantations: Ghosts of Slavery and Legends of the Cotton Kingdom* (Charleston, S.C.: Arcadia, 2007). For a detailed analysis of architectural and material culture in Charleston, see Maurie D. McInnis, *The Politics of Taste in Antebellum Charleston* (Chapel Hill: University of North Carolina Press, 2005).

6. John Berendt, *Midnight in the Garden of Good and Evil* (New York: Vintage, 1994).

7. "Ghosts and Generals: Theatricality, Dark Tourism, and the Ghost Tour Industry," presentation at symposium Future of Civil War History: Looking beyond the 150th, Gettysburg College, Gettysburg, Pa., March 15, 2013. For more on the emphasis that Glassberg references, see Anne Mitchell Whisnant, Marla R. Miller, Gary B. Nash, and David Thelen, *Imperiled Promise: The State of History in the National Park Service*, completed by the Organization of American Historians at the invitation of the National Park Service (Bloomington, Ind.: Organization of American Historians, 2011).

8. Maria del Pilar Blanco and Esther Peeren, introduction to *Popular Ghosts: The Haunted Spaces of Everyday Culture*, ed. Maria del Pilar Blanco and Esther Peeren (New York: Continuum, 2010), x.

9. Jacques Derrida, *Spectres of Marx: The State of the Debt, the Work of Mourning, and the New International* (1993; reprint, New York: Routledge, 1994), xx. Although Hamlet's line about time being "out of joint" can be read as commentary about the political intrigue of the time in which he lived, Derrida interprets it as a theoretical underpinning for understanding the nature of hauntings. See Ann Thompson and Neil Taylor, eds., *Hamlet*, Arden Shakespeare (London: Thompson Learning, 2006), 227, act 1, scene 5, line 186.

10. Avery F. Gordon, *Ghostly Matters: Haunting and the Sociological Imagination* (1997; reprint, Minneapolis: University of Minnesota Press, 2008), 15.

11. Roy Rosenzweig and David Thelen, *The Presence of the Past: Popular Uses of History in American Life* (New York: Columbia University Press, 1998), 7, 9, 67.

12. Carl Becker, "Everyman His Own Historian," *Journal of American History*, 37, no. 2 (1932): 223.

13. Randall Robinson, *The Debt: What America Owes to Blacks* (2000; reprint, New York: Plume, 2001), 15.

14. K. Anthony Appiah, "Identity, Authenticity, Survival: Multicultural Societies and Social Reproduction," in *Multiculturalism: Examining the Politics of Recognition*, ed. Amy Gutmann (Princeton, N.J.: Princeton University Press, 1994), 160.

15. "18% of Americans Say They've Seen a Ghost," Pew Research Center, October 30, 2013, www.pewresearch.org/fact-tank/2013/10/30/18-of-americ (accessed December 21, 2013).

16. Edith Wharton, *The Ghost Stories of Edith Wharton* (1973; reprint, New York: Scribner, 1997), 8. For an early version of Wharton's ghost stories, see Edith Wharton, *Tales of Men and Ghosts* (New York: Scribner, 1910).

17. Gordon, *Ghostly Matters*, 7.

18. Judith Richardson, *Possessions: The History and Uses of Haunting in the Hudson Valley* (Cambridge, Mass.: Harvard University Press, 2003), 3.

19. Renee L. Bergland, *The National Uncanny: Indian Ghosts and American Subjects* (Hanover, N.H.: Dartmouth College, University Press of New England, 2000), 5.

20. Gordon, *Ghostly Matters*, xix, xvi, 206.

21. Philip J. Deloria, *Playing Indian* (New Haven, Conn.: Yale University Press, 1998).

22. Colleen E. Boyd and Coll Thrush, introduction to *Phantom Past, Indigenous Presence: Native Ghosts in North American Culture and History*, ed. Colleen E. Boyd and Coll Thrush (Lincoln: University of Nebraska Press, 2011), vii.

23. Ibid., xi, xiii, ix. On ghost stories as "a technique of removal," see Bergland, *National Uncanny*, xi.

24. Bergland, *National Uncanny*, 9. Alan Henry Rose pointed out the relation between the black and American Indian figure in southern literature, noting that both groups were characterized as demonic in a projection of the racialized psychological fears of white southern society. See Alan Henry Rose, *Demonic Vision: Racial Fantasy and Southern Fiction* (Hamden, Conn.: Archon Books, 1976), 8, 10, 40.

25. Blanco and Peeren introduction, ix.

26. In relating the material that I observed on tours, I have applied the following rule to the disclosure of tour guide identities: When tour guides worked for someone else's company, I used a pseudonym when referring to or quoting them. When tour guides owned and advertised their own companies using their names, I also referred to them by name. When tour guides were aware of my research topic and agreed to speak with me at length and to provide other assistance for the book, I used their names. Some tour guides who wished to remain anonymous are not named or described in the work. Although this book offers critical analysis of historic sites and tour narratives, I have sought to be respectful of individual guides who have a job to do and work hard at it.

27. I use the term "ghost writing" here differently than does Gayatri Spivak, who selects it as an article title but does not delve into a meaning for her usage. Spivak's article in response to Jacques Derrida's *Spectres of Marx* critiques Derrida and other Marxian theorists for marginalizing women. See Gayatri Chakravorty Spivak, "Ghostwriting," *Diacritics* 25, no. 2 (Summer 1995): 64–84. Derrida's *Spectres of Marx* has inspired the language and thinking of cultural studies and geography scholars who study haunting. While I have opted not to emphasize theory in this work, Derrida's influence on this project comes from his insight that ghosts represent temporal disruption. See Derrida, *Spectres of Marx*, xx.

28. Wharton, *Ghost Stories*, 8.

CHAPTER 1

1. "Investigation: Bader's House," bonus investigation, *The Very Best of Ghost Hunters*, vol. 2 (Syfy Channel, Pilgrim Films and Television, 2006). This episode aired on October 31, 2005, as part of a Halloween special filmed in Savannah, *Ghost Hunters*, season 2, episode 14. The interviewees were homeowner Stephen Bader and carpenter Christopher Thomas Bezeredi.

2. See, for instance, Minrose C. Gwin, "Green-Eyed Monsters of the Slavocracy: Jealous Mistresses in Two Slave Narratives," in *Conjuring: Black Women, Fiction, and Literary Tradition*, ed. Marjorie Pryse and Hortense J. Spillers (Bloomington: Indiana University Press, 1985), 39–52, and Mary Boykin Chesnut, *Mary Chesnut's Diary* (1905; reprint, New York: Penguin, 2011), 99–100.

3. Robert Manson Myers, ed., *Children of Pride: A True Story of Georgia and the Civil War* (New Haven, Conn.: Yale University Press, 1972); General Moxley Sorrel, *Recollections of a Confederate Staff Officer* (New York: Neale, 1905). Moxley served

as a captain, then as a lieutenant colonel, and finally as a brigadier general in the Confederate army. His memoir was published in 1905, 1917, and 1958.

4. Sorrel, Matilda, Chatham County Health Department Death Cards, 1803–1893, MS 1717, box 17, Georgia Historical Society, Savannah.

5. Glenn W. Gentry, "Walking with the Dead: The Place of Ghost Walk Tourism in Savannah, Georgia," *Southeastern Geographer* 47, no. 2 (November 2007): 228.

6. Carl Solana Weeks, "Midnight in the Garden of Good and Evil," July 10, 2002, New Georgia Encyclopedia, www.georgiaencyclopdia.org/articles/arts-culture/midnight-garden-good-and-evil (accessed April 12, 2014).

7. John Berendt, *Midnight in the Garden of Good and Evil* (New York: Vintage, 1994), 245, 240, 242.

8. Ibid., 382.

9. Glenna Whitley, "Voodoo Justice," *New York Times*, March 20, 1994.

10. Berendt, *Midnight*, 249.

11. Paul C. Bland, *The Savannah Guidebook: The Essential Guide to Historic Savannah* (Savannah: Coastal Books & Souvenirs, 2010), 4; "Savannah, Georgia: The Lasting Legacy of Colonial City Planning," Teaching with Historic Places Lesson Plans, National Park Service, www.nps.gov/history/nr/twhp/wwwlps/lessons/83savannah (accessed January 18, 2013); "Georgia: Savannah Historic District," National Park Service, www.nps.goc/nr/travel/geo-flor/1.htm (accessed January 18, 2013); Stephen Henkin, "Jewel of the South," *The World and I*, April 1999, 130–37; Gentry, "Walking with the Dead," 228; Karen Hill, "Million-Dollar 'Garden' Home Prices Soaring in Historic Savannah," *Florida Times Union*, November 15 1998, B3; Adam Levy, "Book Bringing Prosperity to Savannah," *Atlanta Journal/Atlanta Constitution*, November 19, 1995, H3. Savannah's original eighteenth-century layout designed by colonist and Georgia founder James Oglethorpe included twenty-four squares; three were lost, and one (Ellis) was rebuilt in 2010, leaving a current total of twenty-two; see Russ Bynum, "Historic Square Resurrected in Savannah, Ga.," *USA Today*, March 15, 2010.

12. Gentry, "Walking with the Dead," 228.

13. Ibid., 224.

14. Amy Paige Condon, "Paranormal Activity," *Savannah Magazine*, April 15, 2013, http://savannahmagazine.com/?s=sorrel-weed (accessed June 5, 2013).

15. Andrew Nichols, email exchange with the author, February 2, 2013.

16. Judith Richardson, *Possessions: The History and Uses of Haunting in the Hudson Valley* (Cambridge, Mass.: Harvard University Press, 2003).

17. A second national original sin is the expropriation of American Indian land, which both expelled native people and produced the desire for increased black slave labor.

18. Deen's first restaurant in Savannah, The Lady, founded in 1970, was later called The Lady and Sons. See Kristy L. Dixon, "Paula Deen," December 21, 2010, *New Georgia Encyclopedia*, www.georgiaencyclopdia.org/articles/arts-culture/paula-deen-b-1947 (accessed April 12, 2014), and Dana Goodyear, "Paula Deen's Ugly Roots," *New Yorker*, July 2, 2013, www.newyorker.com/onlineblogs/culture2013/07/paula-deens-ugly-roots.html (accessed May 2, 2014).

19. Margaret Wayt DeBolt, *Savanah Spectres and Other Strange Tales* (1984; reprint, Norfolk, Va.: Donning Co., 2010), 1. Debolt's book on haunted Savannah has been reprinted sixteen times.

20. William Faulkner, *Requiem for a Nun* (New York: Random House, 1950, 1951 [3rd printing]), 92.

21. For more on how slavery is discussed at public history sites, see James Oliver Horton and Lois E. Horton, eds., *Slavery and Public History: The Tough Stuff of American Memory* (New York: New Press, 2006). Also see Amy M. Tyson and Azie Mira Dungey, "Slavery and Living History," Front Line: Interview with Azie Mira Dungey, *Public Historian* 36, no. 1 (February 2014): 36–60. The release of the feature film *Twelve Years a Slave* in 2013 exponentially increased thoughtful public discussion about American slavery; it should be noted, though, that this was a British film.

22. Leonora LaPeter, "Building History," Savannah Morning News, May 7, 2000, savannahnow.com/stories/050700/LOCsorrelweed.html (accessed March 1, 2012). This article on the Sorrel-Weed House and Stephen Bader pictures the home before the antique furniture was repossessed and paints a more flattering portrait of Bader. See Mary Beth Kerdasha, "The Sorrel Weed House," *Savannah Magazine*, March/April 1999.

23. I was unable to reach Stephen Bader by email or by telephone when I attempted contact in 2012 and 2013. Nor was I able to confirm from staff the date of the inauguration of ghost tours there. I did learn from one staff member via a cold call to the site that the haunting stories started during the "first phase of restoration" in the 1990s. I learned from a different staff member in a cold call one month later that accounts of the home being haunted had started "about a decade ago." This staff member also shared his view that visitors who told personal stories about their paranormal encounters at the home validated the haunting claim. Stephen Bader did not respond to my attempts to contact him. Tiya Miles, phone conversations with Sorrel-Weed House staff members at the site, June 14 and July 1, 2013. Bader and carpenter Christopher Thomas Bezeredi discuss the haunting on camera in the Ghost Hunters First Annual Halloween Special, October 31, 2005; see "Investigation: Bader's House." This is the first recorded documentation that I have found that dates the public haunting stories. Magazine stories cited in this chapter about Stephen Bader and the home from 1999 and 2000 do not mention ghosts.

24. Condon, "Paranormal Activity," 2.

25. Carla Ramsey Weeks, *The Sorrels of Savannah: Life on Madison Square and Beyond* (Savannah: self-published, 2012), 116.

26. Tobias McGriff, *Savannah Shadows: Tales from the Midnight Zombie Tour* (Savannah: Blue Orb, 2012), 109–10.

27. For a detailed and chilling overview of the sexual abuse of black women in slavery based on slave testimony, see Brenda Stevenson, "What's Love Got to Do with It? Concubinage and Enslaved Women and Girls in the Antebellum South," *Journal of African American History* 98, no. 1 (January 2013): 99–125.

28. "Record," document given by Marion Wicko Freyman, Alexander Claxton Sorrel Papers, Southern Historical Collection, Wilson Library, University of North Carolina, Chapel Hill; Sorrel, *Recollections*.

29. Mary Jones to Charles C. Jones, March 29, 1860, in Myers, *Children of Pride*, 571–72.

30. Sorrel, Matilda, Health Department Death Cards; "Funeral Invitation," *Savannah Daily Morning News*, March 28, 1860, p. 2, col. 2; "Died," *Baltimore Sun*, March 31, 1860, 2.

31. Charles C. Jones to Mary Jones, Savannah, Tuesday, March 27, 1860, in Myers, *Children of Pride*, 570–71.

32. Multiple sources indicate that Sorrel sold the home to Henry Weed in 1859: John M. Cooper & Co.'s Savannah City Directory, 1860, pp. 152, 161, Georgia Historical Society; Sorrel-Weed House, Savannah, Ga., Historic American Building Survey No. GA-2140, Index No. GA 26, SAV 48, 1936; Gilbert Moxley Sorrel, "Sorrel Family," First Generation in the United States, Genealogy File, Georgia Historical Society, given by Agnes Sorrel.

33. The Sorrel-Weed Georgia State Historic Site marker recounts the story, also told in Sorrel family biographical papers, that a "faithful slave" saved Francis Sorrel during the Haitian Revolution. See "Old Sorrel-Weed House," Historical Marker Database, http://www.hmdb.org/Marker.asp?Marker=5628 (accessed July 26, 2013).

34. "Copy. Memorandum of Father's Birth, and Baptism," in Aminta Sorrel Mackall, "A Short Sketch of the Life of Francis Sorrel of Savannah Georgia and His Family Tree Down to the Year 1892, Written by his daughter," Sorrel Papers, Southern Historical Collection.

35. Gilbert Moxley Sorrel, "In Memoriam: Francis Sorrel of Savannah, Georgia, 1793–1870," Sorrel Papers, Southern Historical Collection, given by Agnes Sorrel; Sorrel Mackall, "Short Sketch"; Martial Sorrel, St. Mary's Parish, Franklin Louisiana, to Francis Sorrel, Merchant, Savannah, Georgia, translation from the French, November 28, 1885, Sorrel Papers, Southern Historical Collection; Weeks, *Sorrels of Savannah*, 89.

36. Susan Eva O'Donovan, "At the Intersection of Cotton and Commerce: Antebellum Savannah and Its Slaves," in *Slavery and Freedom in Savannah*, ed. Leslie M. Harris and Daina Ramey Berry (Athens: University of Georgia Press, 2014), 44, 48.

37. Moxley Sorrel, "Sorrel Family."

38. Sorrel-Weed House, Savannah, Ga., Historic American Building Survey No. GA-2140, Index No. GA 26, SAV 48, 1936.

39. Slave schedule, City of Savannah, Chatham County, Georgia, 1860, p. 72, Georgia Historical Society, Savannah.

40. Weeks, *Sorrels of Savannah*, 7, 13, 21. Weeks is also author of a historical novel about the Sorrel family; see Carla Ramsey Weeks, *A Single Drop of Ink* (North Charleston, S.C.: CreateSpace, 2012).

41. Leslie M. Harris and Daina Ramey Berry, "Slave Life in Savannah: Geographies of Autonomy and Control," in Harris and Berry, *Slavery and Freedom in Savannah*, 96–97.

42. Janice L. Sumler-Edmond, "Free Black Life in Savannah," in Harris and Berry, *Slavery and Freedom in Savannah*, 130.

43. Ibid., 136–37, 129.

44. For a slightly different analysis of the representation of Francis Sorrel, see Tiya Miles, "Goat Bones in the Basement: A Case of Race, Gender, and Haunting in Old Savannah," *South Carolina Review* 47, no. 2, Spectral South special issue (Spring 2015), ed. Sarah Juliet Lauro and Kimberly Manganelli, 25–36. This essay speculates that Sorrel is not said to be a ghost at his home because of the power of the notion of the black male threat.

45. Sorrel Mackall, "Short Sketch."

46. Moxley Sorrel, "In Memoriam."

47. The collection and organization of documents about the Sorrel family for this project was conducted by Kyera Singleton, a graduate student in American Culture at the University of Michigan; she first pointed out to me the prevalence of mentions of the Haitian Revolution.

48. McGriff, *Savannah Shadows*, 41, 14.

49. Sarah Juliet Lauro and Karen Embry, "A Zombie Manifesto: The Nonhuman Condition in the Era of Advanced Capitalism," *Boundary* 2 35, no. 1 (2008): 97. Lauro and Embry locate the roots of American zombie images (as brain-dead workers and insatiable consumers) in Haitian folklore about the zombie, a being with a soulless body or bodiless soul. They note Haitians' reported sightings of zombielike figures supporting the rebels during the Haitian Revolution; see ibid., 97–98.

50. Robert Edgerly, *Savannah Hauntings: A Walking Tourist Guidebook* (Savannah: See Savannah Books, 2005), vii.

51. Tobias McGriff has sometimes taken patrons to a nearby "Voodoo village," hence the "Zombie Tour" name. The Oyotunji African Village is a community of African Americans who practice the Yoruba faith and carry on West African cultural traditions. Located outside the town of Sheldon, South Carolina, the settlement was established in 1970 as a challenge to and respite from white supremacist American society. See Tracey E. Hucks, *Yoruba Traditions and African American Religious Nationalism* (Albuquerque: University of New Mexico Press, 2012), 167–225.

CHAPTER 2

1. I received an email advertisement from the Hotel Monteleone before Halloween of that year (2013) advertising its haunted history.

2. "The Best Haunted Ghost Tours and People to Meet in New Orleans," Haunted New Orleans Tours, www.hauntedneworleanstours.com/toptenhaunted/toptenhauntednolaghosttours/ (accessed September 11, 2013).

3. T. M. Luhrmann, "Conjuring Up Our Own Gods," *New York Times*, Opinion Pages, October 14, 2013. See also T. M. Luhrmann, *When God Talks Back: Understanding the Evangelical Relationship with God* (New York: Vintage, 2012).

4. Gatherings that were later dubbed "quadroon balls" structured social contact between women of color and white men in New Orleans starting in the early 1800s, offering white men access to a group of women deemed exotic by white Americans. Historian Emily Clark has shown that a great deal of myth surrounds these balls and the intimate relationships that may have been formed

there. A minority of free women of color cohabited with white men in long-term relationships in New Orleans, principally during the Spanish colonial period of the late 1700s. However, many more enslaved women of African descent were used as sexual objects by the white men who owned them, and numerous free women of color were pushed into prostitution or fleeting relationships with white men out of economic necessity or force. In the early American period of New Orleans history, free women of color preferred to marry men of color rather than be with white men in the romanticized interracial liaisons that Karen Jeffries described. For more on the history of quadroon balls and sexual relations in New Orleans, see Emily Clark, *The Strange History of the American Quadroon: Free Women of Color in the Revolutionary Atlantic World* (Chapel Hill: University of North Carolina Press, 2013), 66–70.

5. While the term "Creole" originally referred to anyone born in New Orleans across the racial spectrum, it was later used to denote people of European French and Spanish descent who were born in the colony or whose antecedents were born there. White French- and Spanish-identified residents initiated the change in usage in the Civil War and Reconstruction era because of their fear that the term was becoming associated with people of mixed race or of African descent. See Carolyn Morrow Long, *Madame Lalaurie: Mistress of the Haunted House* (Gainesville: University Press of Florida, 2012), xi, 3.

6. Quoted in Victoria Cosner Love and Lorelei Shannon, *Mad Madame Lalaurie: New Orleans' Most Famous Murderess Revealed* (Charleston, S.C.: History Press, 2011), 21; referenced by Long, *Madame Lalaurie*, 32–33. Long indicates that Delphine's beauty and request on behalf of her first husband, while often attributed as the reason for his pardon due to a reference in the book *Creole Families of New Orleans*, was likely not the actual cause. Instead, Long credits Delphine's husband's letter-writing campaign. See Grace King, *Creole Families of New Orleans* (New York: Macmillan, 1921).

7. Barbara Sillery, *The Haunting of Louisiana* (2001; reprint, Gretna, La.: Pelican Pub. Co., 2013).

8. Love and Shannon, *Mad Madame Lalaurie*, 56.

9. Harriet Martineau, *Retrospect of Western Travel*, vol. 1 (1838; reprint, Carlisle, Mass.: Applewood Books, 2007), 263.

10. Ibid., 264, 265.

11. George W. Cable, *Strange True Tales of Louisiana* (1888; reprint, Gretna, La.: Pelican Pub. Co., 1994), 196.

12. Ibid.

13. Ibid., 200.

14. Ibid., 208.

15. Ibid., 232, 218.

16. Long, *Madame Lalaurie*, 3.

17. Lyle Saxon et al., eds., *Gumbo Ya-Ya: A Collection of Louisiana Folk Tales*, WPA Louisiana Writers' Project (Boston: Houghton Mifflin, 1945), 293, 237.

18. Jeanne deLavigne, *Ghost Stories of Old New Orleans* (1946; reprint, Baton Rouge: Louisiana State University Press, 2013), 257, 252, 253.

19. Barbara Hambly, *Fever Season* (New York: Bantam, 1998); Serena Valentino, *Nightmares and Fairytales: 1140 Rue Royal* (San Jose, Calif.: SLG Publishing, 2007); T. R. Heinan, *L'Immortalite: Madame Lalaurie and the Voodoo Queen* (Tucson: Nonius LLC, 2012). For more on the Hambly and Valentino texts, see Long, *Madame Lalaurie*, 8–10.

20. Love and Shannon, *Mad Madame Lalaurie*, 98, 99, 84–85.

21. Long, *Madame Lalaurie*, 11, 13, 25, 24, 33. Love and Shannon give the date "about 1775" for Lalaurie's birth (*Mad Madame Lalaurie*, 21), as do some websites; Long gives the date March 19, 1787 (*Madame Lalaurie*, 13).

22. Long, *Madame Lalaurie*, 33, 37, 43, 38–39, 48–49, 51, 50.

23. Ibid., 63, 65, 57, 83, 85.

24. Ibid., 67, 69, 70, 71; domestic abuse charge quoted in ibid., 70.

25. Ibid., 89; *New Orleans Bee*, April 11, 12, 1834.

26. Love and Shannon, *Mad Madame Lalaurie*, 45; Long, *Madame Lalaurie*, 136–39.

27. Sillery, *Haunting of Louisiana*, 145.

28. Long, *Madame Lalaurie*, 181–84.

29. Cable, *Strange True Tales*, 202.

30. Diana Williams, "'They Call It Marriage': Law, Race, and Domestic Partnerships in the Nineteenth Century United States" (unpublished manuscript forthcoming from Oxford University Press, 2015), 30–32. Cited with permission of the author.

31. Quoted in Long, *Madame Lalaurie*, 74–75.

32. There were exceptions to this pattern, of course, and sensitive individual white women are sometimes noted with fondness in the narratives of African American slaves. See, for instance, Harriet A. Jacobs, *Incidents in the Life of a Slave Girl: Written by Herself* (1861; reprint, Cambridge, Mass.: Harvard University Press, 1987), 7.

33. Thavolia Glymph, *Out of the House of Bondage: The Transformation of the Slaveholding Household* (New York: Cambridge University Press, 2008), 26, 20.

34. Jennifer M. Spear, *Race, Sex, and Social Order in Early New Orleans* (Baltimore: Johns Hopkins University Press, 2009), 60–61.

35. Ibid., 152–53; Long, *Madame Lalaurie*, 74–77.

36. Walter Johnson, *Soul by Soul: Life inside the Antebellum Slave Market* (Cambridge, Mass.: Harvard University Press, 1999), 2, 6.

37. *New Orleans Bee*, April 12, 1834.

38. "From the Louisiana Advertiser," *New Orleans Bee*, April 15, 1834.

39. Martineau, *Western Travel*, 267.

40. In 1893 the owner of a nearby grocery store, Fortunato Greco, bought the building, advertised on large placards that the house was not truly haunted, and charged ten cents for people to enter and see if they could disprove the haunting stories for themselves. In this way, the creative businessman anticipated a strategy of the popular present-day reality TV show *Ghost Hunters*, where the investigative team goes into haunted buildings purportedly to disprove the haunting stories attached to them. See Long, *Madame Lalaurie*, 161–62.

41. Tim Stack, "Magically Delicious," *Entertainment Weekly*, November 29, 2013, 38. The horror film *Evil Remains* (released October 2004) also borrows from the

Lalaurie story. *Evil Remains* takes place on a cursed plantation founded by the French woman Madame Chevalier. The plot involves the disclosure that the house was burned down by a black slave cook who was chained to the stove. The historical torture of slaves as well as the presence of slave shacks and "spirit jars" set the supernatural stage for modern-day murders that fulfill the historic curse.

42. For a review of the *American Horror Story* third-season premiere, see Chris Jancelewicz, " 'American Horror Story: Coven' Premiere Recap: 'Bitchcraft' Sets the Tone," *HuffPost TV*, October 9, 2013, www.huffingtonpost.com/chris-jancelewicz/american-horror-story-coven-premiere-recap-bitchcraft-b-4060348.html (accessed October 16, 2013).

CHAPTER 3

1. Visit Baton Rouge's Guide, "Historic Plantation Homes," VisitBatonRouge.com Official Travel Resource, 2012 rev.

2. Jill Pascoe, *Louisiana's Haunted Plantations* (Gilbert, Ariz.: Irongate Press, 2004).

3. Ibid., 92–93.

4. Barbara Bader, "Sambo, Babaji, and Sam," *Horn Book Magazine*, September/October 1996, 536, 539; Langston Hughes, "Books and the Negro Child," in *Children's Library Yearbook Number Four*, compiled by the Committee on Library Work with Children of the American Library Association (Chicago: American Library Association, 1932), 109.

5. Solomon Northup, *Twelve Years a Slave* (New York: Dover Publications, 1970); Catherine Clinton, *The Plantation Mistress* (New York: Pantheon, 1982); Robbie Ethridge, *Creek Country: The Creek Indians and Their World* (Chapel Hill: University of North Carolina Press, 2003).

6. Sue Strachan, "Haunted at The Myrtles," www.louisianatravel.com/haunted-myrtles (accessed January 11, 2014).

7. Mark Leonard, senior tour guide, The Myrtles, conversation with the author, December 28, 2013, St. Francisville, La.

8. 1820 U.S. Census, Louisiana, digital images, http://heritagequestonline.com (accessed May 23 2014), citing National Archives microfilm publication M33, roll 31, pp. 43–48 (Eliza Bradford, Clark Woodruff).

9. Rebecca F. Pittman, *The History and Haunting of the Myrtles Plantation* (Jefferson, Tex.: 23 House Publishing, 2012), 112; 1830 U.S. Census, Louisiana, digital images, http://heritagequestonline.com (accessed May 23 2014), citing National Archives microfilm publication M19, roll 33, pp. 238–39; 1850 U.S. Census, Louisiana (Slave Schedule), digital images, https://familysearch.org (accessed May 23 2014), citing National Archives microfilm publication M432, family 265 (R. G. Stirling) and family 413 (Mary Cobb).

10. Mark Leonard, senior tour guide, Myrtles History Tour, December 29, 2013; "Myrtles Timeline," unpublished work in progress shared with the author by Mark Leonard, December 2013; Pittman, *History and Haunting*, 61, 93–94, 112, 118, 120.

11. Mark Leonard, *Murder at the Myrtles Plantation: A Haunted House Mystery* (Scottsdale, Ariz.: Summertime Publications, 2014). Leonard was the senior docent

at The Myrtles at the time that I conducted my research. He informed me that his departure from the site staff in spring 2014 was related to a conflict with the homeowners over the content of his novel. Leonard asked me to read the novel before its publication date. The novel centers around a quirky set of present-day characters fascinated by the mystery of William Winter's murder; it includes hauntings, blues music, Voodoo priestesses, casual sexual encounters, acts of violence against women, and an element of romance.

12. Barbara Sillery, *The Haunting of Louisiana* (Gretna, La.: Keepsake Productions, Pelican Pub. Co., 2001).

13. The Myrtles offers two tours. The Mystery Tour occurs at night and stresses the ghost stories. This tour costs $10 per person and is well attended, with thirty to sixty guests present when I was there. The Historic Tour is offered during the day and is included in the bed-and-breakfast overnight package. It costs $10 for people who have not stayed overnight. This tour focuses on the families who owned The Myrtles in the nineteenth century as well as on architecture and furnishings; it also describes features of the house that were built to protect the Stirling family from bad spirits, such as upside-down keyholes and angel iconography. The family's superstition and protective practices are linked to their Scottish heritage in the tour.

14. Sillery, *Haunting of Louisiana*, 21–22.

15. Saidiya Hartman, *Scenes of Subjection: Terror, Slavery, and Self-Making in Nineteenth-Century America* (New York: Oxford University Press, 1997). Also see this author's compelling travel narrative describing her trip to Ghana as a tourist in search of African American roots: Saidiya Hartman, *Lose Your Mother: A Journey along the Atlantic Slave Route* (New York: Farrar, Straus and Giroux, 2007). For additional treatments of slavery and memory in West Africa, see Bayo Holsey, *Routes of Remembrance: Refashioning the Slave Trade in Ghana* (Chicago: University of Chicago Press, 2008), and Sandra Greene, *Sacred Sites and the Colonial Encounter: A History of Meaning and Memory in Ghana* (Bloomington: Indiana University Press, 2002).

16. Jennifer Morgan, *Laboring Women: Reproduction and Gender in the New World* (Philadelphia: University of Pennsylvania Press, 2004), esp. chap. 1; Deborah Gray White, *Ar'n't I a Woman?: Female Slaves in the Plantation South* (New York: Norton, 1985), esp. chap. 1; Beverly Guy-Sheftall, "The Body Politic: Black Female Sexuality and the Nineteenth-Century Euro-American Imagination," in *Skin Deep, Spirit Strong: The Black Female Body in American Culture*, ed. Kimberly Wallace-Sanders (Ann Arbor: University of Michigan Press, 2002), 13–36.

17. Frances Kermeen, *The Myrtles Plantation: The True Story of America's Most Haunted House* (New York: Grand Central Publishing, 2005), 142, 143, 314–15. Kermeen's description of The Myrtles is in keeping with the classic American haunted house literary form in which the structure itself is tainted or haunted. In the traditional haunted house story, the land and building are personified as evil and intend to harm human residents. This characterization differs from stories about haunted houses that are not themselves alive but are frequented by ghosts who cause trouble. In contemporary American writing and film, the haunted house form and ghost story form are often merged. Of the three homes discussed in this book, The Myrtles most closely fits the classic definition of a haunted house. See Dale Bailey,

American Nightmares: The Haunted House Formula in American Popular Fiction (Bowling Green, Ohio: Bowling Green State University Press, 1999), 5–6, 17, 21.

18. Sillery, *Haunting of Louisiana*, 23, 24, 19.

19. For more on the tragic mulatto/mulatta trope, see Emily Clark, *The Strange History of the American Quadroon: Free Women of Color in the Revolutionary Atlantic World* (Chapel Hill: University of North Carolina Press, 2013), 133–36.

20. Micki McElya, *Clinging to Mammy: The Faithful Slave in Twentieth-Century America* (Cambridge, Mass.: Harvard University Press, 2007), 18–19, 116–17, 120.

21. Kermeen, *Myrtles Plantation*, 61, 68, 143.

22. The description of Chloe as "pesky" is Sillery's in *Haunting of Louisiana*, 19.

23. Minerva is a main character in John Berendt's *Midnight in the Garden of Good and Evil* (New York: Vintage, 1994).

24. Kermeen, *Myrtles Plantation*, 8–9.

25. Patricia Hill Collins, *Black Feminist Thought: Knowledge, Consciousness, and the Politics of Empowerment* (New York: Routledge, 1991), 67.

26. In Sillery's account in *The Haunting of Louisiana*, the features of these two slave women merge such that Cleo disappears from the story entirely and Chloe has the wish to be seen as "a powerful Voodoo priestess" so that "she would be allowed to resume her former standing in the home" (19).

27. Walter Johnson, *River of Dark Dreams: Slavery and Empire in the Cotton Kingdom* (Cambridge, Mass.: Harvard University Press, 2012), 209.

28. Harriet A. Jacobs, *Incidents in the Life of a Slave Girl: Written by Herself* (1861; reprint, Cambridge, Mass.: Harvard University Press, 1987), 28.

29. Ibid., 18.

30. Ibid., 35.

31. For more on placage, see Clark, *American Quadroon*, 66.

32. Gwendolyn Midlo Hall, "African Women in French and Spanish Louisiana: Origins, Roles, Family, Work Treatment," in *The Devil's Lane: Sex and Race in the Early South*, ed. Catherine Clinton and Michele Gillespie (New York: Oxford University Press, 1997), 256, 257.

33. Jennifer M. Spear, *Race, Sex, and Social Order in Early New Orleans* (Baltimore: Johns Hopkins University Press, 2009), 7.

34. See Brenda Stevenson, "What's Love Got to Do With It? Concubinage and Enslaved Women and Girls in the Antebellum South," *Journal of African American History* 98, no. 1 (January 2013): 99–125.

35. Diana Williams, " 'They Call It Marriage': Law, Race, and Domestic Partnerships in the Nineteenth Century United States" (unpublished manuscript forthcoming from Oxford University Press, 2015), 136. Quoted by permission of the author.

36. Myrtles Plantation primary sources are limited and consist mainly of census and vital statistics records of the owners. Chloe is not noted by name in these or in records described in the secondary historical work by Rebecca Pittman. Senior tour guide Mark Leonard declined to include Chloe in his timeline draft document, though he does include her in his tour narratives. I have heard no indication from Myrtles tour guides that Chloe's story traces back to concrete oral histories. One tour

guide who wished to remain anonymous indicated that Chloe's existence cannot be confirmed.

37. Daniel J. Boorstin, *The Image: A Guide to Pseudo-Events in America* (1961; reprint, New York: Vintage, 1987), 11, 79, 103, 106, 108.

38. Historian Stephen Berry, a reader of this book in manuscript form, offered a brilliant analysis of Chloe that can be read as counter to my own and introduces another dimension of Chloe's impact: "Chloe isn't entirely 'ineffectual.' . . . She at least raises the 'specter' of a malevolent rape victim who 'accidentally' murdered everyone her master cared about and, now in spectral form, goes on murdering them every night to the apparent delight of [tourists]."

39. Lyle Saxon et al., eds., *Gumbo Ya-Ya: A Collection of Louisiana Folk Tales*, WPA Louisiana Writers' Project (Boston: Houghton Mifflin, 1945), 273; *Louisiana: A Guide to the State*, Louisiana Library Commission (New York: Hastings House, 1941), 514.

40. Clarence John Laughlin, *Ghosts along the Mississippi: The Magic of the Old Houses of Louisiana* (New York: Bonanza Books, 1961), plate 78.

41. Dottye Varnado, "Ghosts at the Myrtles," *Morning Advocate* (Baton Rouge), May 8, 1960.

42. Spear, *Race, Sex, and Social Order*, 67.

43. Richard Sharpley and Philip R. Stone, "(Re)presenting the Macabre: Interpretation, Kitschification and Authenticity," in *The Darker Side of Travel: The Theory and Practice of Dark Tourism*, ed. Richard Sharpley and Philip R. Stone (Bristol, U.K.: Channel View Publications, 2009), 127.

44. E. Patrick Johnson, " 'Quare' Studies, or (Almost) Everything I Know about Queer Studies I Learned from My Grandmother," in *Black Queer Studies: A Critical Anthology*, ed. E. Patrick Johnson and Mae G. Henderson (Durham: Duke University Press, 2006), 141. For a detailed analysis of contemporary black gay community performance styles, see Marlon M. Bailey, *Butch Queens up in Pumps: Gender, Performance and Ballroom Culture in Detroit* (Ann Arbor: University of Michigan Press, 2013).

45. Johnson, " 'Quare' Studies," 141.

CONCLUSION

1. "Ghosts Among Us," Discover Colonial Williamsburg, www.colonialwilliamsburg .com/plan/calendar/ghosts-among-us/; www.colonialwilliamsburg.com/plan/ special-offers/tavern-ghost-walk-gn (accessed November 26, 2013).

2. Elizabeth Becker, *Overbooked: The Exploding Business of Travel and Tourism* (New York: Simon and Schuster, 2013), 17, 36, 37.

3. John Lennon and Malcolm Foley, *Dark Tourism: The Attraction of Death and Disaster* (Cheriton House, U.K.: Cengage Learning 2010), 3, 11.

4. Richard Sharpley, "Shedding Light on Dark Tourism: An Introduction," in *The Darker Side of Travel: The Theory and Practice of Dark Tourism*, ed. Richard Sharpley and Philip R. Stone (Bristol, U.K.: Channel View Publications, 2009), 11.

5. Ibid., 5.

6. Edward Baptist, *The Half Has Never Been Told: Slavery and the Making of American Capitalism* (New York: Basic Books, 2014), xxi, xxiv.

7. Joshua D. Rothman, *Flush Times and Fever Dreams: A Story of Capitalism and Slavery in the Age of Jackson* (Athens: University of Georgia Press, 2012), 300.

8. Toni Morrison, *Playing in the Dark: Whiteness and the Literary Imagination* (New York: Vintage, 1992), 38.

9. Albert J. Raboteau, *Slave Religion: The "Invisible Institution" in the Antebellum South*, updated ed. (1978; reprint: New York: Oxford University Press, 2004), 4–5, 215, 8, 9, 12, 15, 68.

10. Ibid., 75. It is difficult to differentiate between "voodoo" and "hoodoo" in black life. Raboteau and fellow black religious studies veteran Charles Long define the terms as synonymous in black everyday usage (Tiya Miles, conversation with Charles H. Long, October 2, 2013, Department of Afroamerican and African Studies, University of Michigan, Ann Arbor). See also Yvonne P. Chireau, *Black Magic: Religion and the African American Conjuring Tradition* (Berkeley: University of California Press, 2003), 77.

11. Tracey E. Hucks, *Yoruba Traditions and African American Religious Nationalism* (Albuquerque: University of New Mexico Press, 2012), 11, xiii, xix.

12. Chireau, *Black Magic*, 7, 60.

13. Ibid., 17, 69, 15.

14. Ibid., 154.

15. Ibid., 2.

16. See the classic work on this subject by Jennifer L. Eichstedt and Stephen Small, *Representations of Slavery: Race and Ideology in Southern House Museums* (Washington, D.C.: Smithsonian Institution Press, 2002); see also Antoinette T. Jackson, *Speaking for the Enslaved: Heritage Interpretation at Antebellum Plantation Sites* (Walnut Creek, Calif.: Left Coast Press, 2012).

17. Ella Howard, "Selling the South in Contemporary Savannah," paper presented at the Southern American Studies Association Conference, Charleston, S.C., January 2013.

18. Barbara Sillery, *The Haunting of Louisiana* (Gretna, La.: Keepsake Productions, Pelican Pub. Co., 2001), 17; Jamie Roush Pearce, *Historic Haunts of the South*, Historic Haunts Investigations (Orange Park, Fla.: self-published, 2014), 68. In her history of The Myrtles, Rebecca Pittman debunks the notion that The Myrtles sits on an Indian burial ground and says the Tunica burial ground actually lies beneath the Trudeau plantation down the road; see Rebecca F. Pittman, *The History and Haunting of the Myrtles Plantation* (Jefferson, Tex.: 23 House Publishing, 2012), 49.

19. *Born in Slavery: Slave Narratives from the Federal Writers' Project, 1936–1938*, Library of Congress, Administrative Files, xx–xxii, xxi, http://memory.loc.gov/cgi-bin/ampage?collId=mesn&fileName=001/mesn001.db&recNum=0 (accessed November 20, 2013).

20. Ibid.: Fryer, pt. 1, pp. 339–43; Kilpatrick, pt. 3, p. 12; Kimbrough, pt. 3, pp. 14–15.

21. Ibid.: Heard, pt. 3, pp. 257–58.

22. Toni Morrison, *Beloved* (New York: Plume 1987). Numerous works in the African American literary tradition take up the subject of spirits, haunting, and danger tied to historical racial oppression and subjectivity. See, for instance, August Wilson, *The Piano Lesson* (New York: Penguin, 1990); Randall Kenan, *Let the Dead*

Bury Their Dead and Other Stories (San Diego: Harcourt Brace Jovanovich, 1992); Randall Kenan, *A Visitation of Spirits: A Novel* (New York: Grove Press, 1989); Tina McElroy Ansa, *Baby of the Family* (San Diego: Harcourt Brace Jovanovich, 1989); Tina McElroy Ansa, *Ugly Ways* (New York: Harcourt Brace & Co., 1993); and Tananarive Due, *The Good House* (New York: Washington Square Press, 2003).

23. Elizabeth James and African American Informal Focus Group, New Orleans, February 19, 21, 2014.

24. For an example of a thoughtful as well as moving blog on historic sites of slavery, see Joseph McGill, The Slave Dwelling Project, http://slavedwellingproject .org. The creation of blogs like this one as well as site-specific histories in the form of alternative brochures, websites, and even books made available online or at historic sites can help to augment and enhance the conversation about slavery for tourists. Discussion groups such as the one formed by Elizabeth James in New Orleans for this book can also help to encourage community members' exchange of ideas and information about sites important to their community and city history. Tourists with a strong interest in ghost stories could let the voices of former slaves be among their guides by carrying along collections of preserved slave narratives that treat the subject of ghosts. Doing so, though, would mean recognizing the mediated and sometimes stereotyping nature of these texts, particularly thematic collections of WPA narratives commissioned by state offices. See, for instance, Georgia Writers' Project, *Drums and Shadows: Survival Studies among the Georgia Coastal Negroes* (1940; reprint, Los Angeles: IndoEuropean Publishing, 2010); Ronnie W. Clayton, *Mother Wit: The Ex-Slave Narratives of the Louisiana Writers' Project* (New York: P. Lang, 1990); Lyle Saxon et al., eds., *Gumbo-Ya-Ya: A Collection of Louisiana Folk Tales*, WPA Louisiana Writers' Project (Boston: Houghton Mifflin, 1945); and Lydia Marie Parish, ed., *Slave Songs of the Georgia Sea Islands* (1942; reprint, Athens: University of Georgia Press, 1992).

25. Julia Autry, conversation with the author, West Chester, Ohio, December 24, 2013.

26. Tiya Miles, *The Cherokee Rose: A Novel of Gardens and Ghosts* (Winston-Salem, N.C.: John F. Blair, 2015).

27. Hucks, *Yoruba Traditions*, xxv.

Acknowledgments

I prepared the Brose Lectures for 2015 and wrote this book while serving a three-year term as chair of the Department of Afroamerican and African Studies at the University of Michigan. This was a feat that would not have been possible without the support of many wonderful people. I am grateful to my family, Joe, Nali, Noa, and Sylvan Gone, as well as to Benny, Montroue, Erin and Erik Miles, Deborah Banks Johnson, James King, and Sharon Juelfs, for their support and forbearance. My mother, Patricia Miles King, listened to my reflections during and after research trips and greatly influenced the tone of the book.

I relied on the efforts of terrific research assistants on this project; thank you to Kyera Singleton, Emily Macgillivray, Alexandra Passerelli, Paul Rodriguez, and Michelle Cassidy. I received important feedback on earlier versions of this work from attendees at the Southern American Studies Association meeting in Charleston. Visits to the University of Wisconsin-Madison Center for the Humanities and the University of Chicago Center for the Study of American Culture pushed the project to a higher level. The brilliant readers for the University of North Carolina Press, Stephen Berry and Daina Ramey Berry, offered invaluable feedback and substantially influenced my revision of the work. Although they didn't know it, the fabulous students in my UM graduate seminar on alternative historical writing and my junior seminar on images of African American women constantly inspired me and fed this project, which was under way during the semesters that we had class together.

I am grateful to Bill Blair for inviting me to participate in the Brose Distinguished Lecture Series, which gave this whim of a project a purpose; to Mark Simpson-Vos, a great editor; to Lucas Church; and to the whole UNC Press team with whom I have been fortunate to work on two books. Thank you to the following people who contributed to my thinking in significant ways or otherwise aided the development of this project by ably supporting me: Paulina Alberto (for continual, enlightening dialogue), Farina Mir (for a great insight), Steve Kantrowitz (for a perfect sentence), Sarah Lauro & Kimberly Manganelli (for smart feedback), Beth James (for storytelling genius), Leslie Harris (for Savannah intel), Mark Leonard, Geordie Buxton, Robbie, Piper, Michael, Karen, Tobias, Glen Gentry, Carla Weeks, Ella Howard, Andrew Nichols, Julia Autry, Ashley Finigan, Guy Mount, Stephanie Wichmann, Martha Jones, Meg Sweeney, Dana Nichols, Julie Ellison, Jill Titus, Cherene Sherrad-Johnson, Sharony Green, Ramon Guttierez, Kristin Hass, Kelly Cunningham, Angela Dillard, Liz Cole, Jesse Hoffnung-Garskof, Michael Witgen, Phil Deloria, Greg Dowd, Alyx Cadotte, Adrienne Bombelles, Faye Portis, Tabby Rohn, the faculty and staff of the Department of Afroamerican and African Studies at UM, the staff of the Department of American Culture at UM, former dean Terry McDonald, and the College of Literature Science and the Arts at UM.

Index

African American heritage
tourism, 130
African American religion, 120–22
Aiken Rhett House, 5
Alberto, Paulina, 124
American Horror Story, 76–77,
142 (n. 42)
American Indians. *See* Native
Americans
American Institute of Parapsychology,
28, 29–30, 77
Appiah, Anthony K., 14
Appropriation, 118
Autry, Julia, 131

Bader, Philip, 32
Bader, Stephen, 32–33, 135 (n. 1), 137
(nn. 22, 23)
Baptist, Edward, 118
Bastien, 67
Bastille, 61, 72, 76
Baton Rouge Tourism Office, 80
Becker, Carl, 13
Becker, Elizabeth, 116
Berendt, John, 26–29
Bergland, Renee, 15–16, 17
Blair, Bill, 18
Blanco, Maria del Pilar, 12, 17
Bohemian Hotel, xii
Boone Hall, 6
Boorstin, Daniel, 104
Bourbon Orleans Hotel, 54
Boyd, Colleen, 16
Bradford, David, 86–88, 90, 110
Bradford, Elizabeth, 87
Brown, Johnnie, 129, 130
Buxton, Geordie, 4–8, 12

Cabildo, 56, 68
Cable, George Washington, 58, 63–65,
71–72, 76, 78
Calhoun Square, 44–46
Cannibalism, 60, 62, 124
Catholicism, 44, 51, 57, 64, 78,
109, 122
Cemeteries, 26, 27, 28, 44, 48, 49, 51, 69,
78, 118, 120, 127, 129, 130
Central Georgia Railroad, 38
Charleston, 4, 5–6, 7, 8, 9, 11, 30, 44, 82,
85, 118, 119, 123, 133 (n. 5)
Cherokee, xi, 131
Chief Vann House (State) Historic Site,
xi, 131
Children of Pride, 25
Chippewa Square, 43, 44
Chireau, Yvonne, 121
Chloe, 19, 86, 90–99, 101, 102, 103, 104,
105, 106, 107, 110, 111, 112, 113, 125,
144–45 (nn. 36, 38)
Civil War, xvii, 5, 6, 9, 13, 18, 17, 25, 29, 30,
31, 32, 36, 74, 77, 80, 88, 98, 100, 117,
140 (n. 5)
Clark, Emily, 48, 139–40 (n. 4)
Cleo, 91–94, 98–99, 103, 107, 111–112, 144
(n. 26)
Code Noir, 74
Coldbrook Plantation, 31
Colonial Square, 44
Colonial Williamsburg, 117
Congo Square (New Orleans), 74

Dark tourism, xvii, 9, 43, 70, 82, 83, 99,
112, 113, 115, 116, 117, 118, 119
Deen, Paula, 31
deLavigne, Jeanne, 64

Derrida, Jacques, 12, 13, 134 (n. 9), 135 (n. 27)
Dr. Buzzard, 27, 29
Drayton Hall, 6

EMF (electromagnetic frequency) meter, 4, 60
Epps House, 45
EVP (electronic voice phenomena), 3, 24

Faulkner, William, 31
Feliciana Music Festival, 105
Fischer, Claude, 14
Fleur-de-lis, 107
Foley, Malcolm, 116–17
Francis Marion Hotel, 5
Freedom Trail Black History Tour, 129, 131
French Bedroom, 91–92
Frogmore Plantation, 82, 83, 85

Gentry, Glenn, 9, 10, 11, 12, 28, 125
Georgia Historical Society, 25
Georgia WPA narratives, 19, 126–27
Gettysburg, 9, 11, 29, 44
Ghost fancy, 2, 3
Ghost Hunters / The Atlantic Paranormal Society (TAPS), 2, 9, 22, 23, 33, 37, 53, 106, 109, 135 (n. 1), 137 (n. 23), 141 (n. 40)
Ghost Walk of St. Simon's, 124
Ghost writing, 18, 19, 135 (n. 27)
Glymph, Thavolia, 73
Gordon, Avery, 14, 16, 21
Gray Line Cemetery Tour, 50, 51, 53, 57
Gris-gris, 50, 51, 53, 57, 111, 119, 120
Gullah or Geechee, 7, 19, 118, 119, 130
Gumbo Ya-Ya (Louisiana Writer's Project Narratives), 104

Haint, xiii, 7, 8, 27, 119, 129
Haiti, xv, 22, 34, 35, 36, 37, 39, 41, 42, 43, 61, 78, 99, 120, 121, 129, 138 (n. 33), 139 (nn. 47, 49)
Haitian Revolution. See Haiti

Hall, Gwendolyn Midlo, 102
Hartman, Saidiya, 93
Haunted History Tour, 58, 59, 60, 70, 74, 124
Hoodoo, 121
Hotel Monteleone, 49, 57
Howard, Ella, 123
Hucks, Tracey, 121
Hudson Valley, 15, 30

Ibo Landing, 6
Imperiled Promise: The State of History in National Park Service, xii, xiii, 134 (n. 7)
Infrared thermal meters, 4

Jackson Square, 60
Jacobs, Harriet, 101
James, Elizabeth, 48, 128, 132
Jeffries, Karen, 50, 53, 54, 55, 56, 57, 69, 70, 122, 140 (n. 4)
Jezebel, 94, 96, 97, 98, 99
Johnson, E. Patrick, 112
Johnson, Walter, 100

Kermeen, Frances, 88, 95, 97, 99, 105, 106, 143 (n. 17)
Kermeen, Jim, 95
Kitsch, 107

Lalaurie, Louis, 64, 66, 67, 71
Lalaurie, Madame Delphine Macarty, 19, 54, 56, 57, 58, 60–78, 99, 128, 141 (n. 21)
Lalaurie House, 18, 52, 60, 61, 62, 65, 68, 69, 70, 75, 78, 79, 128
Laughlin, Clarence John, 104, 105
Laurel Grove (The Myrtles), 87
Laurel Grove Cemetery, 26, 129, 130
Laveau, Marie, 29, 51, 52, 53, 56, 57, 66, 72, 76, 99
Lennon, John, 116–17
Leonard, Mark, 88, 90, 91, 92, 93, 142–43 (n. 11), 144 (n. 36)

Little Black Sambo, 83

Lloyd Hall, 82

Long, Carolyn Morrow, 56, 66, 67, 68, 69, 70, 72

Louisiana Courier, 68

Love, Victoria Cosner, 66, 69

Low House, xiii

Madison Square, xiii, xv, 22, 25, 32, 33, 38

Mammy, 72, 83, 94, 97, 98, 99

Martineau, Harriet, 63, 64, 65, 75

McGriff, Tobias, 29, 35, 42–46, 139 (n. 51)

Mercer William House, 28, 29, 46

Michaud, Dolar, 105

Middle Passage, 55

Midnight in the Garden of Good and Evil, 10, 26–29, 31, 32, 33

Midnight Zombie Tour, 28, 34, 42, 43, 45, 46

Millennial anxiety, 117

Minerva, 27, 28, 29, 99, 144 (n. 23)

Mir, Farina, 124

Mississippi River, 48, 60, 80, 81, 84, 86, 88, 91, 100, 102, 103, 111

Molly, xv, xvi, xvii, 1, 3, 12, 17, 18, 19, 21, 22, 23, 24, 25, 26, 33, 34, 35, 36, 37, 40, 42, 78, 103, 115, 125, 130

Monterey Square, 28

Montgomery Square, 44

Morning Advocate, 105

Morrison, Toni, 119, 127

Moss, Jade and Teeta, 106

Moxley, Lucinda, 36, 38

Moxley, Matilda, xv, xvi, xvii, 22, 24, 25, 26, 34, 35, 36, 38, 39, 78, 87, 90

Munson, Marjorie, 104, 105

Myrtles Mystery Tour, 88, 93, 94, 99, 109, 112, 113

Myrtles Plantation, The, 18, 82, 84–95, 97, 98, 99, 101, 102, 103, 104, 105, 106, 107, 108, 109, 110, 111, 112, 114, 124, 125, 143 (nn. 11, 13, 17), 144 (n. 36), 146 (n. 18)

National Park Service, xii, 9, 11

Native Americans, xi, 11, 16, 17, 30, 43, 49, 60, 75, 77, 83, 92, 117, 124, 125, 129, 131

New Orleans, 18, 19, 29, 30, 44, 48–53, 55, 56, 57, 58, 59, 60, 61, 62, 63, 64, 65, 66, 67, 68, 69, 71, 72, 73, 74, 75, 76, 77, 78, 79, 80, 82, 85, 95, 103, 109, 115, 118, 119, 120, 123, 124, 128

New Orleans Bee, 68

New Orleans Picayune, 72

Nottoway Plantation, 80, 82

Oak Alley Plantation, 80

O'Connor, Flannery, 31

Orbs, xv, 4, 12, 42, 46, 47, 131

Ormond Plantation, 82, 83, 85

Owen Thomas House, xii, xiii

Pereen, Esther, 12, 17

Pittman, Rebecca, 87, 88

Placage, 102, 144 (n. 31)

Plessy v. Ferguson, 52

Pseudo-events, 104

Quadroon balls, 54, 55, 57, 139–40 (n. 4)

Raboteau, Albert, 120

Rev. Zombie's Voodoo Shop, 56, 58

Revolutionary War, xv, 77

Richardson, Judith, 15

River Road, 80, 81, 82, 83, 84

Roberto, Paulina, 124

Robinson, Randall, 13

Rootwork, 121

Rosenzweig, Roy, 13

Rothman, Joshua, 118

Royal St. (New Orleans), 61, 62, 63, 65, 70, 71, 73, 75, 78, 128

Ruffin Stirling Room, 89, 90, 91, 106

St. Francisville, 18, 81, 86, 87, 89, 125

St. Louis Cemetery No. 1, 51

Salem, 29, 30, 44, 76

San Francisco Plantation, 80

Savannah, xi, xii, xii, xiv, xv, xvii, 1, 3, 4, 9,
    10, 11, 18, 19, 21, 22, 24, 25, 26, 27, 28, 29,
    30, 31, 32, 33, 34, 35, 36, 37, 38, 39, 40,
    42, 43, 44, 45, 46, 47, 60, 62, 77, 78, 82,
    98, 99, 102, 109, 115, 118, 119, 123, 128,
    129, 130, 131
Savannah Historic District, 28
September 11 attacks, 11
Shannon, Lorelei, 66, 69
Sharpley, Richard, 9, 10, 107, 117
Sillery, Barbara, 58, 69, 70, 95, 96
Solitude Plantation, 91, 111
Sorrel, Aminta, 40
Sorrel, Francis, xv, xvi, xvii, 22, 24, 25, 26,
    34, 35, 36–41, 78, 99 138 (nn. 32, 33),
    139 (n. 44)
Sorrel, Gilbert Moxley, 25, 36, 41
Sorrel-Weed House, xiii, xiv, xvi, xvii,
    1, 4, 11, 12, 17, 18, 19, 21, 22, 23, 26, 32,
    33, 34, 35, 36, 40, 41, 42, 46, 78, 79,
    103, 115, 130, 137 (nn. 22, 23),
    138 (n. 32)
Spear, Jennifer, 103
Spivak, Gayatri, 1, 135 (n. 27)
Stirling, Mary Catherine Cobb, 87, 91, 112
Stirling, Ruffin Grey, 87, 89, 90, 91,
    106, 112
Stone, Phillip, 107
Supernatural, 2, 6

TAPS (The Atlantic Paranormal Society).
    See Ghost Hunters
Telfair Museum of the Savannah School
    of Art and Design (SCAD), xii, xiii
Thelen, David, 13
Thompson Robert, 9, 10
Thrush, Coll, 16
Titus, Jill, 9, 11

Tragic mulatta, 96, 97, 144 (n. 19)
Twelve Years a Slave (slave narrative,
    film), 83, 84

Vann, James. See Chief Vann House
    (State) Historic Site
Vesey, Denmark, 5, 6
Voodoo, xv, xvi, 27, 28, 29, 37, 42, 43, 44,
    45, 46, 48, 49, 50, 51, 52, 53, 56, 57, 58,
    59, 62, 63, 65, 72, 76, 77, 78, 79, 88, 91,
    93, 95, 98, 99, 106, 107, 111, 113, 118, 119,
    120, 121, 122, 126, 130, 139 (n. 51),
    146 (n. 10)
Voodoo dolls, 107, 122
Voodoo priestess/queen, 27, 55, 91,
    99, 107, 111, 113, 143 (n. 11),
    144 (n. 26)

Weeks, Carla, 29
West Africa, 52, 62, 139 (n. 51),
    143 (n. 15)
West Feliciana Historical Society, 81, 88
Wharton, Edith, 14
Williams, Diana, 103
Williams, Jim, 27, 28, 29
Winter, Sarah, 88, 93
Winter, William, 87, 88, 93, 143 (n.11)
Woodruff, Clark, 87, 90, 91, 92, 94, 96,
    102, 103, 110
Woodruff, Sarah Matilda Bradford, 87,
    90, 95, 96, 111
Wormsloe Plantation, 46
Wright, Jenny, 35

Yellow Fever, xiii, xv, 44, 77, 87, 91, 93
Yoruba, 42, 44, 115, 121, 139 (n. 51)

Zombies, 2, 43, 46, 63, 66, 139 (n. 49)